Peace
By
Piece

Peace
By
Piece

Tessa

PEACE BY PIECE

iUniverse books may be ordered through booksellers or by contacting:

iUniverse
1663 Liberty Drive
Bloomington, IN 47403
www.iuniverse.com
1-800-Authors (1-800-288-4677)

Because of the dynamic nature of the Internet, any web addresses or
links contained in this book may have changed since publication and may
no longer be valid. The views expressed in this work are solely those
of the author and do not necessarily reflect the views of the publisher,
and the publisher hereby disclaims any responsibility for them.

Any people depicted in stock imagery provided by Thinkstock are
models, and such images are being used for illustrative purposes only.
Certain stock imagery © Thinkstock.

ISBN: 978-1-4917-6725-2 (sc)
ISBN: 978-1-4917-6726-9 (e)

Print information available on the last page.

iUniverse rev. date: 04/14/2016

This book is dedicated to all victims and survivors of abuse.

Only God can ease your pain and give
you true peace in your soul.

Foreword

(AS YOU READ THIS BOOK, PICTURE YOURSELF
AS AN INFANT, 2 YEAR OLD, ETC.)

The following incidents are based on my life and are true to fact. I am a 54 year old incest survivor. Due to a multitude of incidents, other health issues, and an imbalance of my brain chemicals, I have been diagnosed by several doctors with the following: Depression, Bi-Polar II (Manic Depression) with Psychotic Features, Post Traumatic Stress Disorder (PTSD), Schizoaffective, Suicidal Tendencies, Homicidal, Self-Mutilation, Body Memories, Dissociation, Emotional Detachment, Distortive Thinking, Agoraphobia, Diabetes II, Lymphocytic Colitis, Essential Familial Tremors, Left Bundle Branch Block- LBBB (heart issue), panic/anxiety attacks, and hypothyroidism. I also had Bells' Palsy in 2012, however, it went away in approximately a month. Doctors have estimated my depression began at around five years of age.

At some point in my adulthood, I found myself engulfed in the midst of an horrific abusive cycle that had been compounding for many years. I came to realize that the first real step to be taken in shattering this pattern was to recognize and take control of it – and to stop letting IT control me. This would be the hardest job of my life (ongoing still). But I intend to get there.

When I meet someone new, one important thing I learned is to keep my past to myself for a while. It boils down to the fact that I've lived with this for 54 years and have had a long time to try to deal with this: how can I expect to tell someone else about my past all at once and have them understand when they have no clue how to deal with it. Trust me, this can cause bad reactions from someone you could have had a truly good relationship with.

If people in general don't acknowledge to themselves that they're caught in an abusive cycle, they can't possibly escape and conquer it. I consider this to be applicable in all types of abusive situations, regardless of if they are physical, emotional, sexual, etc., or related to drugs, alcohol, etc.

Hopefully this writing will allow others to see that there is a way out. Never give up on life and, if you have to, force yourself to realize that there is real hope and that your life really can improve. Life is what you make of it and true peace and happiness are attainable. There's a saying – 'fake it till you make it'. At times I still tend to forget this myself. I feel like it's never ending abuse. But I keep trudging along. There is a light at the end of the tunnel, even if you can't always see it.

Table of Contents

Chapter 1

Background

<u>Maternal</u>

When I was 15, I learned that my grandfather had molested my mother when she 13 years old. He high-tailed his backside out of town when confronted by my grandmother. I must commend my mother for telling my grandmother. It was very brave of her, especially when people snub you as an outcast. It was very difficult and taboo to speak of these happenings during those years when such issues weren't acknowledged.

My grandmother began to frequent bars and covert with her lovers, sometimes several at a time, literally. She was an extremely beautiful woman. Considering the horrors she had to deal with and her internal turmoil, I'm sure it was the only way she knew how to survive the horrible way this trauma had affected her. However, she couldn't see through the fog and consider her children at this point. She needed to survive.

My mother was the oldest of six children. At the young age of 16, she married my father. He was 21 and in the Air Force. He eventually moved her to his home state. My mother's five younger siblings were raised by relatives, an orphanage, and/or foster care.

My mother was young, inexperienced and had no self-esteem due to her horrific past. Accordingly, she was evidently unaware of how to face the world. This understandably led her through many years of heartache and denial in attempting to deal with her own past (let alone even noticing mine). I felt so all alone.

Please don't think I hate my mother. We never bonded when I was a baby/child/teen/adult. She's been living with me for the past four years, since about when I turned 50. Bonding started a bit at a time more recently. There are issues which we have been working on, without stating so, for these past several years and are making huge steps in the right direction. I love her very much. She was so young getting married that she hadn't had time to grow up herself. And her father should have been castrated for his actions. But, again, we have forgiveness.

Paternal

My father, I've heard, as a child was thought to have been molested by his father. He had extremely long gaps in his childhood that were completely void of memories.

Parts of him must have been OK. I saw how people treated him. He was loved by every one that I noticed. They liked his sense of humor and he generally seemed to be a good person, except when his dark side was showing, not in front of others.

At my great-grandfather's funeral, my father introduced me to his cousin (who was also his uncle). My great-grandfather had raped his step-daughter and they bore a son, who is the cousin/uncle. Why would he only tell me this? I found out later that he never even told my mother and that it really was true. Did he just feel the need to try to freak me out?

An aunt told me, when she was young, that my grandfather (her father) raped her, too. She went to live with a relative. She still was having nightmares in her 70's and, until his death, used to hide if he came to her house when her husband wasn't home. She would lay low until he would finally leave.

I was also told that my paternal grandmother slept in the room with her youngest daughter until she was 13, in order to protect her.

2

Once when I was small, I was trying to look in their bathroom mirror. It was too high for me to see in it. My grandfather walked by and picked me up so I could see. My grandmother walked by and started screaming at him to put me down. From that day forward, I thought she hated me and I felt extremely unloved by her. I had already lost my self-confidence. As an adult, I began to understand that maybe she was trying to protect me from him. Maybe she loved me that whole time. I wish she would have lived longer so I could have gotten to know her. God bless her soul.

With a family history like this one, what is the chance of having a healthy childhood? Not a real self-esteem booster. How many more uncovered secrets are buried deep within? God is pulling me out of the pit of our family tradition. More forgiveness? Yes.

How do I love myself
Let me count the ways
Mmmmm??
Can't seem to find one right now

Help Me

I'm crying out for help
Isn't anybody there
I really need to talk
Doesn't anybody care

Just for a little while
I have to figure myself out
Everything is building up
Someone help me out

Doesn't anybody care
Come and rescue me
I'm drowning in myself
This is a desperate plea

Don't you care a bit at all
For a person who's really down
Can't you tell that I need help
By looking at my frown

If not – look into my eyes
What do you see there
The spark is almost gone
It's mostly a blank stare

If someone could just help me
This isn't a child's game
To straighten out my messed up life
And turn my soul back to a flame

Chapter 2

Daddy's Little Girl

As a little girl, friends would sometimes ask silly questions of each other. "Who do you have a crush on?" or "Does he like you, too?" In later years, the questions were harder. "Are you still a virgin?" or "When did you lose your virginity and with whom?"

Those dreadful questions always scared me. I always try to be honest. I hate lying. This was the perfect time to go for a 'potty break'. I would get emotionally and physically sick. How do you answer questions like that when you can't ever remember even being 'pure'?

I didn't have a 'normal' childhood – from what I've seen and/or heard from other people. My father committed horrible acts. Of course, it didn't help that my mother worked nights to be away from him (due to his abuse of her) and, in my opinion, was in some type of denial (my definition – the only sure way to survive your own personal pathway through hell). I don't think she could have dealt with it.

I can remember sitting in my dark closet trying to hide from the horror. I would cover myself with clothes and shoes to not be seen. I would stare into the darkness with my eyes wide open and pray that no one would find me. If I heard footsteps, I froze…

I have definite gaps in my childhood. Good memories just don't usually come to me. However, the terror never lapses from my subconscious. It seemed that the terror was always there just waiting for the chance to attack me. I was sooo afraid to tell, to run, of being killed. I WAS ALWAYS SO AFRAID. A new link had just been added to the chain of the abusive cycle I live in.

Don't all little girls want to be "daddy's little girl"? After all, he's the man every little girl should be able to look up to – her protector, her provider. Therefore (about three years old), when he told me to come over and sit on his lap, I did. The problem was that I was too young to know it was wrong and that my dad would hurt me. By the time I realized doing so was a mistake, it was too late. His game had started…approximately from infancy into my adulthood, still attempting until his death.

I would be in my pajamas, ready for bed, when he would call me to come sit on his lap. Don't all dads have their own recliners? He leaned back with me on his lap. He began patting my legs then, very slowly, he inched his hand up.

The next thing I knew, he was fondling me. OVERWHELMING FEAR, FROZEN, NUMB, FEELINGS OF MY OWN DEATH. When he finally let me up, he made sure I knew it was my fault. He would remind me to – 'Never let him do that to me again'. LET HIM? As if I was in control of anything at the young age of around three. I would walk away feeling the fear of death if I ever opened my mouth. He knew how to make me feel at fault, and oh so guilty.

My mother told me, as an adult, that when I was around 2, my father would tell me to come kiss him goodnight and then refuse and I would go to bed crying every night. And his nickname for me, growing up, was 'fat butt'. I had always felt fat growing up. Most of my family on that side were overweight and got picked on a lot. That I remember. It added to the breakdown of my self-esteem drastically.

Again, with my mom working nights, no one was there for me at the time. Thinking back, my biggest fear at the time was that I couldn't remember how long ago this had started. I can remember many of these incidents by the time I was two or three years. The memories kept me in constant fear. In later discussions with my mom, it was determined that these and/or similar incidents must have been initiated in my infancy. He would never change my brother's diapers, but always wanted to change mine. Molested/fondled as an infant - sick b*****d.

Another thing to remember – always check your window blinds before changing for bed. It was another disgusting, horrifying shock to me when I discovered that immediately before I was told to go change for bed, my dad would sneak in my room and raise the blinds to go outside and watch me change my clothes. I finally caught him once, leaving my room. I asked what he was doing. He just looked at me and walked away. Then he told us to go get ready for bed. I heard the front door open and close. When I went in my bedroom, I searched for anything different in there. The blinds had been opened about a foot. I thought I would drop over dead. How long had this been going on?! Overwhelming humiliation flooded my soul yet again. How does a child fight the devil? For that's how he appeared to me.

He eventually started coming in my bedroom in the middle of the night or early morning. Those were the worse times. I couldn't even make a guess at how many times this happened.

I tried to keep him out. Of course, I didn't have a real door. It was a bamboo-like sliding door. I would tie the cloth belt off of my robe from the makeshift door to a dresser drawer knob. I also set my trash can in the doorway so he would trip on it if he tried to come in. Of course, none of that would keep anyone out. I was just a child trying to protect myself. I also remember, when I was beginning to develop, how he would make me hug him tightly into his body and I would cringe when he called me 'peaches' and said I was 'his girl'.

When he would come into my room, I would be asleep and he would start by fondling me then work his way around to other sexual acts. It scared me to death and hurt me so much physically.

I also remember him forbidding me to close the bathroom window when showering to prevent the mirror from fogging over. We lived out in the country and didn't have a cover for the small upper window. Yeah – I figured it out eventually. I still have flashbacks and nightmares – sometimes he lets his friends watch me, too, in the nightmares. I don't know that his friends really watched. So, now I'm adamant about making sure my house all is closed up by dark. It's too easy for anyone to see in… And keep your doors locked and close the curtains! Even during the daytime.

When I was two, at a holiday dinner in our house, my mom caught one of my older cousins raping me (two years old!). My mom didn't know what to do, so she did nothing. It was family – five brothers. They were very good at sharing, if you know what I mean. Since there were no repercussions, it was evidently deemed apparent in their minds that there would be no backlash, which led to gang raping multiple times until I got old enough to know it was wrong and learned to fight back.

I remember at four years old, knowing what oral sex was – not the name, just the act. I spent long periods of time hiding, in bushes, in trees, and in my closet. I wrote a lot.

Prior to me knowing that it was wrong, when I was around five to eight, I had sex with two neighbors, brothers, occasionally. It was nothing out of the ordinary for me. I had been raised being used to thinking that it was normal and that's how you show someone you like them. As soon as I knew it was wrong and had the physical ability, I stopped it from happening ever again.

However, my father never quit trying. When we moved, my senior year of high school, I had to go to a school where no one talked to me all day. Depressed me again. So I told my dad

I wanted to go to school where my cousins were. He tried to get me unclothed and get into bed with him so we could 'work it out'. The attempts ended when his life did.

For some reason, it's extremely harder for me to feel actual forgiveness when incest is involved. This man was supposed to provide for and protect me as his child, not perform sex acts to me or on me. It's illegal and definitely disapproved of by family and social guidelines.

I've heard in therapy that it's normal for some molestation victims to be frigid and some to be hot for sexual encounters. I am one of the hot ones. A good friend of mine from work had been molested by her brother as a young girl. As a wife she said she'd rather hire her husband a prostitute than have sex with him herself. But they were very much in love. I, on the other hand, wanted it more all the time. It messes with your mind.

The Abuser

No one ever asked me to come out and play
But I wasn't a child in our house anyway
I always felt the need to run and hide
For all I really knew was fear inside

If others were near they'd be hurt too
So I shut myself down and no one knew
I couldn't be part of the world and face
The shame, disgust, and loneliness

I was hurt and felt so unsure
I couldn't remember ever being pure
I had suffered so much abuse and pain
That there seemed to be nothing left to gain

I wanted a person I could tell all to
One who really cared and would be true
But no friends could ever be made or met
As I sat alone in my dark closet

Was real trust and caring ever there
I wondered as I woke from another nightmare
Now I don't know what emotions I can feel
And I can't remember if I'm real

Maybe hope once filled my eyes as I looked at you
But none of the "love" you gave me was true
Now my eyes are empty and my heart is sore
But my soul keeps searching for something more

God gave man free will to do as we please
But He saw what you did and He wept with me
The judgment will be your burden to bear
And God will see to my love and care

I pray the Lord my soul to keep
As again I cry myself to sleep

Chapter 3

Childhood

I grew up in the country. There were about four houses in a row (an old row of houses for the coal miners and families – half were unlivable), then nothing but cow pastures and corn fields. We were across the road from an old coal mine and a small wooded area. I remember making fire pits in the woods. Something I enjoyed.

When my parents bought our home, they didn't realize there was no toilet in the bathroom. Out back there was a two-seater outhouse. It was scary going out at night with a flashlight to find my way around. I usually woke my sister up to go with me.

We also had a manual water pump outside. Sometimes we had to use it for water. There was not adequate plumbing in the house.

I remember in the winter melting snow on the stove for a bath or dishes. We were only allowed to use about six to eight inches of water in the tub. With three kids, we had to use the same water. Last one had dirty, cold water. I tried to always go first; it was on a first come basis.

There was also a coal room in our basement. A coal truck would fill the room with coal using a chute. We had to shovel coal into the furnace for heat.

We eventually got a toilet in the house and an updated furnace. However, with the plumbing in the house being so poor, we could only flush when it became full of excrement. It still overflowed quite often.

We had an old ringer washer but no dryer. I had to take a kitchen chair outside so I could reach the clothes line to hang clothes to dry. In the kitchen, I also had to stand on a chair to reach for washing dishes at around six to seven years of age.

We had a party line telephone. If the people we shared the line with were talking, we had to wait for them to hang up to use the phone.

In the mornings, my mom would be getting off work and my dad would be going to work. We had to be outside when the bus came or the driver wouldn't stop. The route passed by about ¼ of a mile down the road. So, if we hurried, we could catch it there. Otherwise, we missed school that day. I remember missing the bus one day in a snow storm. We had to walk ¼ mile to the next stop and my feet and hands hurt with a pain like you couldn't believe. I felt like my fingers and toes were on the edge of frostbite and was sobbing. The teenager at the house let us stand in the garage – but not the house. It was better than no shelter at all. I just kept crying until I could feel again.

I had a friend when I was around 10 years old. She lived in a fatherless home with her siblings and her mother, who was busy working all the time. She stayed overnight once. We slept in sleeping bags on the living room floor. I woke up in the early morning and saw my dad in the kitchen making coffee and getting ready for work. He looked at me with a blank look and turned away. I turned and looked at her. He had opened her sleeping bag and pulled her nightgown up around her neck. She was almost naked. I didn't see what just happened. She obviously didn't wake me or say anything to me. Subconsciously, I knew immediately what he had done to her and I felt overwhelming fear and shame and didn't know what to do. And now, as an adult, I probably would have killed him if I could. I was a child in fear for my life.

The next school day, I saw her in the hallway. She started screaming at me in front of everyone. I hadn't seen that one coming. I guess I wanted it to all be just a bad dream. She yelled that she hated me and never wanted to talk to me again – SCREAMING. My emotions were flooding my heart which was being torn in half. I loved my friend and hated my dad. And all my schoolmates in the hall between classes were just staring at me. It was one of the worst days of my life. I felt devastated and embarrassed and never did talk to her again, as she had requested. I heard years later that she became a stripper and had two children. I've always wondered if the molestation had a roll in her choices in life. And it hurts my heart to think so. But how can I take responsibility for what my dad did?

I talked to another friend several years ago. She told me that, when we were young, my dad took her for a ride on his new motorcycle and molested her, too.

That was about it with having friends. I stopped inviting them over. It wasn't worth losing friends due to my horribly perverted father! These practices may take place in other countries, but not ours!

I started working at 12. I baby sat on a regular weekly basis. I saved all the money I could.

At 13, I was working out in the fields. Kids would ride on a bus and go out in the fields to 'detassle corn' in the heat of the day. And they were steaming days, sometimes over 100 degrees. (Very hot and draining work.)

At around 14, a different neighbor raped me in one of my hiding spots. I tried to fight him off, but he was older and stronger. He laughed when I told him I would scream. He said he knew I wouldn't because I was too timid, afraid, and embarrassed. He was right. Luckily, I didn't get pregnant… I stayed away from him as much as I could.

At 14, I 'walked beans' with an old farmer (family friend) weeding the fields in the heat of the day. (Again very hot and draining.)

Another neighbor, one of my best friends, told me he always loved me. At 16, he proposed to me. I told him I thought of him more as a brother. Evidentially, that's the wrong response. He was pretty upset. We'd been in school together since kindergarten. He eventually joined the service and begged me to come with him. I didn't go. After the fact, he married a girl from another country and they had three children. I wish the best for him and his family. One of his sisters was one of the victims of my dad's molestation. His other sister died from cancer, years later. The man she married was the above mentioned neighbor/rapist. Life is so cruel and twisted sometimes.

When we got in trouble back then, dad would make all three of us pull our pants and undies down around our ankles, lean over the bed, and whip us with a belt. I don't think we needed to be half naked to get the whippings. Occasionally he would have us go pick out our own switches from the trees – the green ones (they hurt more) and give us some welts with them.

One summer we went to a Bible Camp with some neighbors. Everyone was praying loud and strong. Some were using different languages. I didn't understand. All of a sudden I felt myself coming out of a trance-like state and I was speaking in a different language, too. Freaked me out. Later I learned that was what happened sometimes when you are filled with the Holy Spirit. And some people do it all the time. I haven't since. It was a good learning experience. I know it's real!

Some neighbors moved in down our old dirt road – about ½ mile. When I was 15 or so, I got a new best friend. To this date, I still love her best of all. She was a God send in the middle of my own private hell; my escape from the reality of my life. Without her, I don't know what I would have done. We always stayed the night at her house, obviously. I never told her anything about my 'private' life.

Sometimes I would burn myself with cigarettes or try to overdose with aspirin. Self-mutilation seemed OK at the time. I was a total wreck. But I was a good pretender, with many different masks.

I put all my attention into school work and had all good grades. As a senior, I had a GPA of 3.968. I just tried to be away from my home as much as possible.

My best friend had a boyfriend and he had his best friend for me. We all hung out for several years, until we moved out of state. I never gave myself to him, even though he was my boyfriend. He was also my first loser. Didn't work, didn't call, etc. I thought this was normal, too.

At 16, I took a little time off working in the summer. Mom, my sister, her friend, and I went on vacation. Two of my uncles, at different times, tried french kissing me. One at his house and the other in a swimming pool while wrestling underwater. I know they had bad childhoods, too. Again, forgiveness. I can't get caught up in it anymore. All together, these happenings were too much to handle. One of my favorite uncles, was recently deceased – due to cancer treatment. Too much radiation and/or chemo. He didn't die from the cancer but from the treatment.

Eventually, at 17, I went to work at a nursing home as a Dietician's Aide. I remained working there until we moved out to another state later that same year. It was hard to leave all the people I had grown so very fond of. They were more like family than my own.

My somewhat boyfriend moved after us shortly after we left. He was staying with us. He made several mistakes, drinking, loafing around, not working, and got booted out by my dad.

He did call twice when I was about 30. We talked the first time about the relationship we used to have. The second time he called, he had a buddy with him and they both wanted to come here and have a threesome. Big H*** NO. That's the last time I talked to him until I recently had contacted him on-line. He looks like Charles Manson's brother. He's claims to be an ordained minister, has remained celibate for seven years, has Hep C (which is untreatable in his case), and is just biding his time to go home (heaven?).

<u>Free</u>

We gaze at the stars above
Looking into the past
And wonder how much longer
This world will last

Traveling from this universe
Our minds see many new things
And they wonder all of their lives
How we fly without wings

There's so much of life to live
We'll never experience half
Orion looks down on us all
Using his sword as a staff

We yearningly float to the sky
And look down as their world does
Asking why some can see through
And wondering – what was the cause

Open your mind and see
And your soul can climb and be free

Chapter 4

Holiday Blues

The house was filled with the aroma of the golden-brown turkey baking in the oven. I'd never cooked Thanksgiving dinner before, and the only reason I was doing so now was with my roommate for his children. And actually he was the chef and I was only acting as his assistant.

My family doesn't get together anymore. Too much pain and uncomfortable, I guess. But my mother, when she was working, came by to eat before her shift started. She came over early to help. She made the unintentional mistake of shifting the kitchen table at an angle, as a space saver. Big mistake. My mother and I had never bonded and didn't really know each other at that time. If we had, she should have been able to question me about my reactions.

I felt petrified with terror. I was on the verge of losing my mind.

I flashed back to a holiday dinner long, long ago. We were at my aunt and uncle's house. After dinner, the adults told the kids to go somewhere and play. Those cold winters forced us to retreat to the basement. I was about five years old then. One of the five cousins, all boys older than me, forced me behind the couch – which was set at an angle – as a space saver I imagine. He raped me as his brothers watched and stood as lookouts. When he was finished, he traded places with another brother. This continued, their 'train' or 'gang-bang', until they were all finished. I was, and still am, completely filled with disgust, shame, and degradation.

I can't have furniture set at an angle in my house! I learned a new lesson about myself that day. More currently, this doesn't seem to bother me as much, since I understood what had made me sense fear.

We periodically went camping and fishing with the same family. This was the last time I remember them trying to force themselves on me. One of the cousins started making advances toward me. I was scared to death but took a deep breath and told him NO. But the cousins didn't give up easily. If nothing else, they would gang up and try to pressure me into something. He grabbed me by the arm and dragged me over to the other brothers. He told them what he wanted to do to me, and that I wouldn't let him. They surrounded me and goaded me. "Come on. She'll let me do it. Come here. Let me stick my hands down your pants." Over and over they all provoked me. Run little girl, run hard and fast; and don't look back.

It seems that I couldn't get away from my cousins. Every time I knew I had to see them, I felt myself freeze with fear and dread. Now I wonder how any parent could let their child live through that hell. Especially when you know at least one person in an authority position knows some things that have occurred. It only stopped when I was old enough to defend and protect myself.

Remember

Remember the times when I was small
And Christmas time was here
That's the time we were all around
The ones we held so dear

Every year we went to Grandpa's house
And all the relatives would arrive
Those were the very happiest times
When Grandpa and Grandma were alive

The men sat in the living room
Told stories and talked of old times
While all this time the women cooked
Wonderful food and delicious pies

All the kids would get together
And think of games to play
We all had so much energy then
We could go past the end of day

The women called when time to eat
And we'd all go get in line
Grab a plate and pick out food
There were so many different kinds

The men would go back to the living room
While the women stayed to clean
They told the kids to stay out of the way
And go out to play again

We'd all bundle up and go out in the snow
It was all so sparkling white
We played tag, built big snowmen
And best – had snowball fights

Then the time came to go back in
None of us argued – but went
The time had come our Grandpa said
To pass out the Christmas presents

Grandpa sat down right in front of the tree
Picking out presents one by one
All the kids waited with big, round eyes
And when your name was called – what fun

After the presents were all passed out
We'd all play with our new things
Then we'd stand around Grandpa at the organ
To joke and laugh and sing

Then the kids were all put to bed
In the other room for a while
The parents relaxed in the living room
And sat talking of the day with a smile

That was the way it as back then
My, how times have changed the family
But we'll always have those happy memories
And we'll cherish them eternally

Chapter 5

Mom

After the death of my father, my mother admitted to me the knowledge of the bedroom incident when I was two. She said she wasn't aware of any of the other problems. I lost control when she told me about that. If something would have been done the first time, all the other times may not have occurred if there was supervision. What about the innocent little child? Who was there to protect her? NO ONE.

Needless to say, birthdays and holidays have never been an easy time for me. They're like dark clouds. They trigger my depression and surround me like an itchy, wool blanket, which I can't breathe through – suffocation and anxiety attacks.

My mother and I, as I mentioned, never bonded. Now that she's been living with me for the past four years, we've started to bond as adults. It's a slow process and sometimes we need a break, but I think we've accomplished a great deal during this time. We've come a long way. If we couldn't have the lost child bonding, at least we can work on an adult bonding relationship.

Childhood

(As it should be)

You kissed me when I hurt
You held me when I cried
You babied me when I was sick
And punished me when I lied

The many things you did for me
When I was a child
Are appreciated much more now
And helped my life become styled

You kissed me when I was hurt
That taught me to care
You also taught me other things
Like why and how to share

You held me when I cried
And made things all seem better
You told me that you loved me
Then nothing was the matter

You babied me when I was sick
With custard, love, and hot tea
The couch was soft, the TV low
And I felt all that mattered was me

You punished me if I told lies
That helped me most of all
You taught me about discipline
So I'd live my life with less falls

You taught me to be independent
And let me be myself
Now I love being on my own
And try to do it well

Chapter 6

Sweet 16

I had always heard that turning 'sweet 16' was supposed to be a very special day for girls. As a result, I had some grandiose, ludicrous dream of a wonderful party, friends, and acceptance, etc. The dreams were of satin and lace, femininity, pretty pink things, boyfriends, the road to becoming a woman, and such. My reality was nowhere near this fantasy visualization.

At 15, I was working on a school work permit at a local hotel, restaurant, and lounge. I made money to buy some school clothes, my guitar, eye contacts (kept me from being called four-eyes), and started a savings account. Of course, I had to rely on others for transportation since I was too young to obtain my own driver's license. Mom was still working nights, which led me no other real options. My dad drove me.

Occasionally a co-worker would give me a ride home. One night I accepted a ride home after a long shift (1:30 am). I was very shy and naïve – never even dated. But I had a crush on this "older guy" who offered me the ride. He was a college student who worked at the restaurant for his uncle during the summers. He seemed so nice and polite that even my best friend's mom (who also worked there with us) liked him. She later said that she'd been hoping he would ask her daughter out.

I directed him way out in the country to our old dirt road as he drove me home. When we reached the point where I pointed out our house, he sped past our house for several miles. I was raped that night in his car. At some time during the assault, I blacked out and came to in a sort of zoned out shock mode. During the attack, I recalled a car driving by very slowly. This was extremely out of the ordinary at the time and place, a dirt road with no houses, in the middle of nowhere. Obviously he didn't want to kill me or dump me in a ditch, and he proceeded to drive me back to my house. In the trance-like state I was in, I got out of his car and walked into the house.

My dad was waiting up for me. He asked who drove me home. He pointed out that my belt was unbuckled. I clammed up. He didn't have anything else to say so I just went to bed.

After three days of continuous bleeding, I was consumed with the fear of bleeding to death, pregnancy, etc. Due to my mother's over emotional tendencies, I felt I could only approach my dad, and I needed to go to a doctor. During her graveyard shift, she wasn't there for me to tell anyway.

I gathered every ounce of courage I possessed and decided to talk to my dad. In my mind, he would tell her, she would calm down, and she would take me to the doctor – end of story. No such luck! His reaction completely blew my mind, causing another severe crash in any type of self-esteem that I was trying to gain for myself by being out in the world.

He asked me if a car drove by during the rape. I said, "Yes. Why?" He didn't respond. That frightened and angered me at the same time. Wouldn't you expect him to stop and help – especially if he's your father???!!!

He proceeded to inform me that you can't get pregnant unless you enjoy it and have an orgasm. Then he wanted to call the police and file a report. I told him if he called them, I would slit my wrists. I couldn't deal with the emotional strain on myself, at only 15 years old. (I had just seen a movie in which they made the victim look like she was a slut and was asking for it. She was treated like a whore.)

Then he told me to undress and lay down on his bed with my legs spread so he could examine me himself. He said he wanted to know if I was bleeding on the inside or the outside.

I totally lost it. I was in a daze, hollering and crying. I could not deal with any of this anymore. This hurt me more than the rape I had just gone through. I couldn't trust my dad for anything.

I ran from his room to my cubby-hole bedroom. I was consumed by a plethora of emotions so horrible that I cannot find the words to express the deep pit I was sinking in. I felt huge waves of guilt, fear, disgust; you name it. I totally realized that his car was the one that drove by during the rape and he had not stopped to help me. I was very modest and not sexual. I believe, even if I was being consentual (which I was NOT), my father should have protected me from myself, never even had a date before. My father seemed to have an odd feeling of possession toward me. I believe he wanted me to be his whenever the thought hit him. I also fully recognized the fact that my dad wanted to use my misfortune as an added opportunity for his perversion. (In later years, I told my sister and she said she had always wondered what had happened to me that night, hearing me yelling at him.) My heart crashed to the ground. I hadn't expected much of him, I admit. But I thought wrong. Little did I know that I was opening up another door into that sick, demented world of his.

After the fact, he did tell my mother about the rape. She made an appointment with an unknown doctor (for privacy, I'm sure). She called the school and told them to have me outside at a certain time for her to pick me up.

When I got in the car, she broke down. I just knew this would happen. I had wanted to avoid it. I was so tired of always feeling like I had to be the strong one (emotionally). I needed love and understanding.

She proceeded to tell me she completely understood how I felt. When she was 13, her father molested her. She told her mother, who immediately confronted her father. This led to the disappearance of my grandfather for 24 years. I met him when I was 17. He had changed his identity.

I silently listened to her sobbing as she told her story and could only feel anger at what I thought was her, and my own, self-absorption. I didn't think she cared enough to help me. Inside I was screaming, "LOOK AT ME DEEP IN MY EYES. DO YOU SEE THE PAIN? I'M GOING THROUGH A CRISIS AND AT THIS TIME CAN'T COMPREHEND THE COMPARISON OF HOW MY FORCABLE RAPE AND MOLESTATION WAS AFFECTED BY YOU AND YOUR PAST. HOW DID YOU SURVIVE? I WAS YOUR BABY GIRL. WHAT ABOUT MY DAD AND ALL OF MY OTHER ISSUES (COUSINS & NEIGHBORS & SUPPOSED FRIENDS)? I CAN'T TELL YOU THAT PART. HE WILL KILL ME. WHO'S THERE FOR ME?" (No one, as usual. God will guide me through my catastrophic life.)

I understand my mother's plight. However, this all started with me as an infant and had never been addressed. I always wanted a protector. My mother had the guts to tell her mother (who believed her). I never had the guts to tell anyone. I was afraid of being killed.

I kept my mouth tightly shut on the ride to the doctor's office. He suggested I file a police report, also. The bleeding was caused by my having been torn inside. He prescribed me an anti-bacterial medication and sent me on my way. None of this was ever mentioned about this incident again in my family.

The bleeding finally did stop. Then I went without a period for four months. When it came back, there were huge clots of tissue, blood, and a lot of pain. At a later doctor's appointment, he determined it was a miscarriage. My angel baby would have been 38 years old by now. Under the circumstances, God must have meant for this to be.

Then – I turned 16. But everyone had their minds on other upsetting issues at the time. My mom remembered my birthday several days later. Too much drama had filled our heads. There went that special birthday.

The rape issue got out around at work. He told everyone I willingly had sex with him. But that would never have happened. I was too afraid of sex and pregnancy, etc...

Several months later, as I waited for my dad to pick me up, I was seated in a waiting area by the front doors. I began to feel sick to my stomach and unexpectantly began shaking with apprehension. I didn't know what was going on. My back was to a hallway. I think God was warning me that something was going to happen. I jumped as I felt someone's hand touch my shoulder. I turned and looked up straight into the face of my rapist. I was bewildered with shock and couldn't react. How dare he even approach me. He bent toward my ear and quietly said, "I'm sorry." Then he turned and walked away. I just sat there in stunned silence. Now, no matter what the other people thought, he had just admitted his guilt to me. And I could hold my head up just a little higher (no more staring at the ground around others). It was a very bitter-sweet vindication.

He's Always There

When the sorrows of my life have got me down
And I can't find anyone around
You draw me near and lead me home
And all my fears are gone

You walk beside me all the way
Your presence tells me what words can't say
You saw my tears and wiped them dry
And chased the clouds from my sky

If only I'd seen just how blind I've been
You have always cared
And you've always been there
I didn't have to search anywhere

You were always standing right by me
You were just waiting for me to see
The happiness that's mine
Was always right before my eyes

Unending Love

He smiles at me each and every day
He takes my hand to lead me the right way
With nothing left for me to live for
He opened up a whole new door

He came on a dove
To show me His love
A pure white dove
With His unending love

Life goes by with its ups and downs
But He gives me hope when He sees that I'm down
How did I live without Him for so long
He fills my heart with His own sweet song

He came on a dove
To show me His love
A pure white dove
With His unending love

He made my life worth living again
He's who I need – And He'll be there through the end
I'll always get by with Him helping me
There's so much more He's got for me to see

He came on a dove
To show me his love
A pure white dove
With His unending love

Chapter 7

God

I am nothing without you!!!

Shout with joy to the Lord.

I remember my mom taking us to church when we were very young. We were told Bible stories and sang children's songs. I remember my parents fighting about going to church. My dad never would go. But she definitely introduced me to God. Ever since that time, I have known God was with me and Christ is my Savior. Then we just quit going for some reason I'm not sure of. But the basics had taken hold; the seed had been sown.

I remember crying and praying and hiding. And all this time, I knew God was with me. I didn't know why I was living this way, but I knew that He was with me and would take care of me. As a teenager, I went to Church every time I could – Sunday AM, Sunday PM, and Wednesday PM. I was baptized in the Raccoon River. We would memorize Bible passages and go sing at retirement homes and the state hospital. I had a friend who would sing duets with me to my guitar. I would talk to my friends – in their hearts. Maybe I got lucky and helped to plant some seeds.

God held me in his arms so many times. He sheltered my soul through all the evil doings against me. He saved my sanity. When I sat in my dark closet, he wept with me and gave me the strength to live.

More To Give

When I was a child I hid from life
I only knew pain – felt fear and strife
No one kept me safe from harm,
though they knew it was there
No one kept me safe – as if no one cared
I wanted to end it all you see
But a bright light shone down on me

"Child – look into my heart and see
There's happiness in store for thee
I gave my life for you to live
And you've got so much more to give."

But now my life seems clenched with fear
I try to live for now, but the past is still there
With my man by my side and my son's hand in mine
I hope that peace can finally be found
I pray to live my life the right way
Because I can still hear Christ softy say

"Child – look into my heart and see
There's happiness in store for thee
I gave my life for you to live
And you've <u>still</u> got so much more to give."

THE GIFT OF LOVE

He gave us the gift of love and redemption
Through his unimaginable suffering and pain
And although we can never repay Him
We can receive eternal life as the gain

He had the power to lay down his life to save us
And the power to get it back through our Living God
Love one another; no one gets to the Father but by Christ
Father forgive them for they know not what they do, He said

Darkness came as the Messiah's spirit left his broken body
The earth quaked as it gave up his human form
His body was released and placed in a tomb
Leaving His followers lost and forlorn

He rose from the dead and made himself known
He ascended to Heaven like a dove
Eternity is ours when we are saved
Made possible by his sacred love

Jesus of Nazareth, a carpenter by trade
He cured the sick and made whole the blind
He was a prophet, a teacher, a healer
Making Heaven the goal you can find

Christ

Christ hung on Calvary's cross
That dark and dreary day
And when the people cried to God
He said He'd show the way

Just believe in my Son Christ
Who died upon the cross
Whom I sent so you could live
Despite My horrid loss

He loved you all so very much
That He died quite readily
And He didn't beg His Father above
Where He knew He could safely flee

Always pray for His forgiveness
And His everlasting love
Which was sent down from Heaven
On the wings of a snow white dove

Tell Him you love Him and follow His will
Help other people for Him
And each day Heaven will get brighter
As the dark earth will get more dim

Someday you'll pass through the pearly gates
And cross the streets of gold
You'll be there all through eternity
And for Christ you'll always be bold

Chapter 8

Brother

My brother and I are 'Irish twins'. This obviously is not actual twins, but siblings that are born less than a year apart. We're the same age for ten day every year. He is older and we are very close.

My brother married when he was in the Navy. When he was 22 and their son was about six months old, his wife stabbed him in the heart in his sleep. She ran out of their apartment partially nude, accidently locking herself out. A neighbor took her in, thinking she was being molested. My brother became alert enough to make his way down the hall to the living room and call 911. He passed out on the couch. They came by helicopter. When they beat on the door, he woke and opened the door. Then he passed out again.

He had no blood pressure left and had to have emergency open heart surgery. His lung had also collapsed and they said it was a miracle he survived. My parents and I flew out to see and help him. My parents were granted guardianship of my nephew.

My brother recovered and stayed with his wife another seven years or so. He took back custody of my nephew. His wife and her family had failed to tell my brother that she has Paranoid Schizophrenia. After the incident, he stayed with her; she had a relapse and was admitted to a psych hospital. They later divorced.

He continues to be drawn to needy women, some who were very 'off the wall'. Some were very seriously abusive to his son, him, and/or themselves. The worse one put a lock on the outside of my nephew's door and made him use an empty coffee can for a toilet at night. She also made him put on shorts and kneel on sugar on a piece of newspaper for an hour, until the grains dug into his knees. She wouldn't move out – so he had to sell the house to get rid of her.

My brother eventually remarried (a different woman, of course). She had two children and was looking for a stable man to take care of them all. He already had a son. They had a daughter together. He also found out that he had a son as the result of a one night stand. A DNA test was done. He adopted his step-daughter, but not his stepson (whose father was deceased). He ended up being the father of five. When they divorced, he paid child support for three of the children.

He has always had very good jobs. At this point, he has custody of the youngest and all they others are legal adults. The youngest one just graduated and just found out she is pregnant. She moved in with her older sister and they intend to raise the baby girl. My brother has to learn how to be alone for the first time in years. He has a very comfortable income and does very well for himself. He also has two grandchildren (beautiful).

At 51, my brother had a heart attack and had to have a stint put in his heart. He was also told he has diabetes. Early stages (takes pills). The doctors have given him a clean bill of health.

He's been married twice, many other relationships, and is still looking for a good woman. I wish for one for him, too. He's a good man.

My brother's position was eliminated and he was laid off. He put one of his houses up for sale. He's having a massive yard sale and is flying somewhere for an interview. Good luck to him. I'd love it if he moved back here. He came out to visit on the 4th of July. We had a great time.

<u>US</u>

We grew up together
And loved each other much
And when he decided to go away
We made sure to keep in touch

We shared some good times
And some bad ones too
We laughed and cried together
With all that we've been through

But he's more than just my brother
He's a true and close, dear friend
And even though we have our differences
He will be there til the end

Chapter 9

Sister

When I left the house for good, at 18, I told my sister about the incidents with our father. She told me about him grabbing her breast and trying to french kiss her. Obviously, no one was safe around him.

She was not a morning person and I remember physically pulling her out of bed while she kicked and yelled at me. But it's the only way I could get her out of bed for school.

I had so many bad feelings and frustration going on in my head that I could not control - I had to walk through her room to get to mine. (My room had a single bed and dresser with just enough room to walk between the two.) I would put my arm out and swipe everything off of her dresser. I had so much internal pain that I couldn't get it out any other way at the time. I have apologized to her and hope and pray that she forgives me.

She moved out of state and stayed with my parents for a while. My dad let one of her friends stay with them until she got back on her feet. My sister found her crying on the curb one day. My dad had sexually assaulted her. He told her that nothing comes free in this world. Would he ever stop?? My sister confronted him on the phone. He played stupid.

My sister has been divorced three times. Like myself and my brother – drawn to the wrong type of person (due to our childhood abuse?). No children were born to her.

My sister has a beautiful soul. She has a boyfriend (14 years) and will do almost anything for anyone in need that she can. She has an amazingly good heart. She's been taken advantage of many times, but she has also been blessed by God many more times over. I love her immensely. My baby sister.

Earth Angel

God gives us someone special
Only once in a while
And when one comes along
You see it in their smile

She's always there for me
And cheers me in all trouble
She'll help in any way
She steps in on the double

This time I was lucky
God gave me one this time
She's always there to help me
And leave you feeling fine

But the blessing will be theirs
Whoever knows her well
For my sister's always there
An angel sent to help

Chapter 10

Husband #1 - Roy

My last day of high school, I moved in with Roy. It was a very bad move on my part, but it did get me away from my dad (which was extremely worse to me).

Anything – yes, I would have done anything to leave the house, that I should have been able to call a home. I met Roy while ditching high school. I was 18 and he was 36. He was a biker and had a mean look about him. That's what drew me to him. My dad would never bother me again. I thought I'd be safe now. Little did I know that his anger would eventually turn on me. - This is not a reflection on bikers. Most of them I know are wonderful people and loyal friends. And he wasn't an alcoholic or drug user, just mean.

I had a Siamese cat who was in heat. The howling got to him and he went and got his gun. He aimed it at the cat and I yelled, "Don't shoot my cat!!!" So he turned to me and put the loaded gun against my temple and said, "OK b****. I'll shoot you!" I froze. I didn't move a muscle or say a thing. Roy took the gun down eventually. It scared me to death. But I never told him that.

Sometimes he would hit me or throw things at me for no apparent reason that I can recall. He would just get mad and assault me. He also threw me down a flight of stairs. I went unconscious and woke up with him carrying me to the bed. I think his actions were starting to scare him, too.

One time we were at a friend's house. He got really mad at me for a reason neither of us remembered afterwards. He punched me and called me a f****** c*** in front of their whole family.

I just took off walking, weeping and SO embarrassed, with nowhere to go at 3 am. I eventually went back to the house we were visiting and things had settled down some by then. We went home.

Roy also, at another time, pushed me to the floor and started kicking me in the sides and banging my head on the floor. There were many other physical and emotional abusive occurrences. Sometimes I had visible bruising. People at work always asked. I didn't talk. I was so embarrassed. Bruises fade (but aren't forgotten). Words never go away. He used every nasty word there is at me and I'm sure I responded in the same manner. He was my first and I thought it was normal.

We bought a house together. But the physical and verbal abuse continued. I thought it would stop. Duh. I didn't think I could get away. It eventually got the best of me.

My cousin and I went out one night – and so did he, separately. When we were at home and went to bed, Roy leaned over to kiss me goodnight and I smelled a female's vaginal secretions in his beard. I went off on him. He never denied it.

He told me to get out. I got my purse and my guitar. He followed me to the front yard. He knocked me down, kicked a hole in my guitar and dragged me by hair back into the house. He shut all the windows and blinds, unplugged the phone, and locked the house up. I suffered a mental breakdown, sat shriveled up in a corner in the living room crying silently and engulfed in fear and not understanding why things had gotten so bad and what to do. I was so scared at 21.

I waited until Roy had to go to work and called my relatives. They were SO helpful. I love them very much and will never forget the help they gave me. They (uncles, aunts, and cousins) all brought over their vehicles and moved me out. My things went into storage and I moved in with my cousin. We are the same age and were very close back then.

He blew the engine in my car. I had to get rides to work until I could afford a car. I signed a Quit Claim Deed on the house to him. I just wanted out.

He started harassing me. He called me at work and threatened to blow up my new (very used) car, in the employee parking lot. He threatened my life. I was very afraid. I had to report these threats to my boss, they were so bad.

We had no children. The divorce was easy. I processed it without an attorney, through the county.

I heard that Roy was eventually put on psychiatric medication for his issues and was doing better. Years later I heard he passed away from cancer. All is forgiven.

I wonder at the forgiveness of myself, additionally. It seems to me that I will never forgive myself. I see my faults and problems every time I look in the mirror. I am very codependent.

I think that I was more forgiving with the other people in my life rather than my father. In my mind, he was supposed to be my protector. I think it's also harder for me because it was incest. We are blood related. There are so many women willing to have sex, why did he have to choose me?

Doubts

Love has its doubts
For you and me
But sometimes I think
I should just flee

I tell you I love you
And think it's the truth
But people say I'm mixed up
Because of my youth

But when I tell you of my love
You don't say very much
You just smile and give me
A friendly little touch

All our friends disapprove
It shows in some faces
But they can't understand
Cause they can't take our place

And the confusion arises
Again and again

Chapter 11

Husband #2 - Joe

My cousin and I went out a lot. What will a lonely woman do for companionship? Another man who fell in love with me. It was mutual. The chemistry was there.

Later - Joe was full of lies – compulsively. He is the biological father of my son. He told so many lies that I'm sure he started to believe them himself.

Once he was fired from his job and didn't tell me. He left every day and came home at a normal time. One day, when he was 'working' I found the letter stating that he was terminated, dated several weeks prior. I think that's when he started cheating on me with strippers. One of his friends, who wanted to be with me, got drunk and came to tell me. I also caught him in a bar once dancing with a stripper (off duty – had clothes on). I told him to quit lying or leave. He was out the door in record time. Joe left me with nothing but a sick baby, bills, and heartache. There was an eviction notice on the door, a car in my name that he took, and bills that had stacked up. My son was on oxygen for six months and had 'failure to thrive' for another year, not growing properly for his age group. My son eventually caught up and is a wonderful, normal person above average health wise.

My family came to my rescue again. The county was sending me to a Safe House. There were so many roaches at the safe house that they didn't even run when we turned on the lights. I couldn't stay there for my son's sake (or mine). My aunt let us stay at her house until I could get on my feet. My dad (the only time in my life that he helped me) wired me $1,000 which

I paid back as fast as I could. That's how I had the money to buy an old used car that ran good.

I had almost all of my belongings in the car, covered by a sleeping bag. At work one day, another employee asked me if I was working out of my car at night. That broke my heart some more... Another employee stated that she would NEVER date someone who was divorced. There I went. I asked her if her husband had ever held a loaded gun to her head. That stopped the discussion very quickly, but was another stab to me.

When Joe (my son's biological father), had left my son was eight months old. I asked him for $10 to help get diapers once and he told me NO. He told me he had gone to the doctor and had stomach cancer. He said his boss was so concerned about him that he wouldn't let him come back to work without a doctor's note because he was so ill. I called his boss. They told me he wasn't employed there anymore because he didn't come to work for three straight days, with no communication, and they wanted proof that he was sick, because they also thought he was lying. He never showed up again.

I found a roommate, coworker, and we got a two bedroom apartment. I had a large walk in closet and that's where the crib went. I lived in those apartments for seven years. After a year she moved out and joined the service. Luckily my Section 8 kicked in at the same time. I had enough income that I didn't qualify for food stamps, however it was low enough to qualify for Section 8 Housing. They paid for half of my rent. Thank God. Now I could afford staying on my own and my son had his own room.

Other incidents to mention are as follows. Joe and I took my parents on a drive in the mountains and passed a herd of buffalo. He stated that there were 350 buffalo out there. I got in trouble because I questioned his knowledge of this. He said he saw it on TV. Liar, trying to impress my parents and it backfired on him.

Joe told me he was going to play football. He said we were invited to a dinner with the big wigs. He then said he hurt his ankle and wouldn't be able to play, conveniently before the dinner.

Another time, when I made him mad, he hit me and gave me a bloody nose. I'm sure I said something wrong – pushing his buttons. Then he got out of car and punched my front windshield.

Rather than looking back and trying to place blame on each other, I look more at who can control their violent actions. My previous therapist (retired) said I was brainwashed as a child and that I am drawn to that type of man.

Before I met Joe, he went AWOL from the Marine Corp and was arrested in his mother's yard in front of all the neighbors. She told me she was horribly embarrassed. I received this information from my ex's mother.

Once, when I was about eight months pregnant, we got in a fight and he said he was leaving (don't remember what about). We only had my car. I asked where he was going. He said to the store and I asked if he would wait for me to get my purse to go with him. He said OK. When I came out, he was long gone and didn't come home until the next day. Pregnant, massively depressed, and crying. I was just wondering if he learned that he could pick a fight just so he could walk out on me. Another time he was gone for 2 days.

The night I gave birth, after visiting hours, Joe went to a strip club. He lied about it, but had written a check there. I worked in a bank and had them look up who the check was to. He told me it was a down payment for a mother holding a child statue for me. It was payable to cash but had an endorsement on the back from the strip club. He wasn't covering his tracks very well and didn't realize I could find some things out.

When Joe claimed he had cancer, I got the name of the hospital and doctor. His health insurance was through my job. I called to investigate his information. No such doctor. No such admission, etc…

After our divorce, when he got another job, I applied for his child support to be garnished from his wages and his IRS refunds. He quit his job the same day his check was garnished. Child Support only got one IRS return and he quit filing. They said that he either changed his identity, was working under the table for cash, or doing his best to disappear in any manner he could.

Joe hasn't tried to contact me ever again. He never even called to see his son, who is now 28 years old.

I recently located him through a computer agency. It had his address, phone number, and wife's name listed. I filed against him at the County Courthouse. I sent the papers to the Sheriff's Department in his county. They served him. He appeared at court on the hearing date and was ordered to pay or go to jail for up to six months. He offered to pay $250 monthly until paid off in 2019. It was stopped by the time my son was adopted by my third husband, but still adds up to just over $18,000.00. The judge approved the payment schedule and I'm just waiting for the first payment. If he doesn't pay it, they'll put an arrest warrant out for him. He told me he can't go to jail, so I'm pretty sure he'll pay.

Just checked the mail. Got my first child support payment and it only took 26 years. Joe's current wife sends me checks monthly and has been very good about keeping everything caught up.

Forgiveness? Still there, hopefully on both sides.

Joe's mother just passed away (2013). She suffered from MS for many years. She was always very good to me. I used to call her once in a while and send pictures of our son and grandson. I will miss her not being there.

Done Trying

Just when happiness is within my grasp
It seems to slip away
And if that chance will come again
Who can really say

If I had kept my heart at a distance
I'd have never felt the pain
But between loneliness and a chance at love
Would it have been a loss or gain

I'd never try to hold you back
From what you feel the need to do
But the heartache that it caused me
I didn't need from you

Chapter 12

God's Intervention

I took my son to visit my parents when he was around two years old. I thought my father would NEVER try anything again. But I couldn't have been more naive or wrong.

My son and I went on a Greyhound bus to spend two weeks at my parent's at Christmas time. Another bus broke down and we had to take on all their riders. Being Christmas time, everyone was openly welcoming the new people. It was very crowded but no one cared.

At my parents, my son and I slept in adjoining bedrooms. We went to bed at a decent time. I was in a very sound sleep. I felt someone sit down on the edge of the bed. You know, how you can feel the mattress dip? I came half way awake. No one was there. I slipped back into my somewhat peaceful sleep. All at once, a light brighter than any I've ever seen flashed in my head. I sat straight up, very alarmed. No one was there. It was around 3:00 am. But I watched as the bedroom door was opened and my father started to enter the room. Still sitting, I yelled at him asking what he wanted. He said he just wanted to tell me goodnight. I yelled NO. We had already done that hours before. He walked out and shut the door. I surely was afraid of what would have happened if God had not been there to protect me. The angels surrounded me and I slept peacefully the rest of the night. I was never so glad to go home from any vacation. I was 27 and he still couldn't act like a good father.

Never Alone

Your still small voice within me
Helps me when I'm down
And You'll give me a smile
To take the place of my frown

You give me friends in people
And an even greater one in yourself
So that when I'm lonely
I'm never by myself

You take away all my fears
And replace them with a calmness
Which can only come from you
So my weary mind can rest

You tell me not to worry
Everything will be alright
And somewhere in my future
You see a shining light

Life holds something special
As everyone's must hold
If it takes awhile
Someday we'll all be told

There's More Beyond

On the other side is a breathtaking
Glorious celestial land waiting
Crossing the great divide is fate
But there we will have no murder or hate

Christ lives on the other side
Some will pass away as others abide
He said there is nothing to fear
So don't you shed a single tear

It will be a place you'll not want to leave
And with a future like this you'll yearn to believe
You'll love the pearly gates and the golden streets
But best of all you and He shall finally meet

Don't ever give up on life my friend
Christ will be there even after the end
And when your own special day has dawned
You'll see after all – there's more beyond.

Chapter 13

Husband #3 - Ross

I walked into the neighborhood bar and noticed a new face. A friend introduced me to his nephew. From there – things flew.

Ross and I immediately began seeing each other. We both fell for each other very quickly. My son was only three and slightly apprehensive because he didn't know him. But they bonded very quickly. My son loves him with all his heart.

We got married in a Chapel. It was beautiful. We were so in love.

After a year of marriage, adoption can take place. We were all so happy. The judge let my son sit up on his desktop and asked him if he wanted Ross to be his daddy. He was only six years old and loved him so much. He, of course, told the judge yes. All was wonderful at that time.

We tried to get pregnant, and did. We lost that baby (would be 27), died invitro. We were both so heartbroken. I had to have a DNC or chance an at home miscarriage. If I chose to just go home the baby might not miscarry and would calcify causing surgery. So I chose the DNC. Life went on.

About six months later Ross and I tried again. We got pregnant. A year to the day, we miscarried (would be 26). His sister was pregnant, too, due 2 weeks after ours. Her baby was beautiful and is gorgeous. August 31st was our bad day. Again, life went on.

He was the love of my life. I think we withdrew from each other due to the miscarriages and my depression. And my son has never forgiven me for divorcing Ross. Even so, his father remarried and has been with his current wife ever since. He has a wonderful wife and I pray for their continued happiness. They just bought a house and he also just had both hips replaced.

The Fear

You told me long ago
We'd never part
But I've told you may times
No one will ever own my heart

You float beside me
On the sea of life
And you walk right by my side
Down each road of strife

You've been the best friend
Anyone could be
But my heart keeps telling me
I've got to be free

You say you'll wait for me
To forget my pain
That you have nothing to lose
And I have everything to gain

Love

You've got my heart in your hand
And have since we first met
You've got a certain something
That makes my love grow yet

You said people have to start out slow
And we'd be friends for a while
But somehow it didn't work for long
The love came through with your smile

The way you look at me with those eyes of yours
Makes me feel you see my every thought
And when you say you love me so very much
I think I'd want to die if you did not

You're always so kind – it's hard to believe
You consider me all of the time
You're not like all those other men
Who want you and just throw you a line

The flowers you send and gifts you give
Didn't make up for how you lived
I packed my bags and decided to go
And leave the life that we had shared

There were just too many things
Which had happened that I couldn't bare
We'd started fighting a lot
You don't understand so how can you care

I cried when I found out
That my memories were too strong
The past had caused me such emotional pain
That I didn't think it would last very long

Some old love of your life called almost every day
She said she wanted you back
And you didn't know what to say
So, I'm the one who had to pay

I loved you and lost you
Was it my fault or yours
I loved you and lost you
When I walked out the door

I guess that I just wanted more
But what am I looking for

My Love

You're as gentle as a sea breeze
But as strong as the sea
And my wish upon a star
Is to have you all for me

My love for you is deep
It flows both night and day
And the feelings so strong
I'll die if you ever go away

I love you with all my heart and soul
Remember these words so true
Cause some things I can't say too well
So keep in mind my love for you

The light of love shines in my eyes
As people pass by my way
They wonder at my smiling face
As I think of you each day

I couldn't bear to let you go
You brighten all my dark skies

I love you so ----
I see the sun rise and set in your eyes

Life

I live alone in a lonely world
And live the best that I can
I've got to search and find myself
A good loving man

You know I've roamed the streets at night
And slept on many a floor
But that's not half enough for me
I'm going to get myself more

The moonlit beach is always there
To comfort all my sorrows
But now I've got a true friend
To help me through all my tomorrows

He helps me when I'm feeling sad
And he helps me when I'm down
And when we feel like going out
Together we hit the town
****

Now our son is grown and gone
And he's got a child of his own
So now we'll remember all of our dreams
And all the others we've sown

Chapter 14

Me

Hide. Don't know what else to say, etc. And my experiences have helped to develop me into an extremely compassionate person. I care about everyone and am very empathetic. *I am not a victim. I'm a survivor.* Emotional trauma has to go.

Today I'm so unsure of myself. I'll have to watch and see if this is a cycle. One day depression, the next uncertainty?

More denial?

My mother continually skirts the issue of her awareness. She swears to have no knowledge of any problems at the time. Yet, she admits to being aware of my depression and resentment at an extremely young age (around age 6). We talked about denial. We then discussed that this was the reason she started working nights and my father started to visit my room. Of course, I remember earlier abuse; sometimes it was during the daytime when anyone could have seen, but no one did. I inquired whether or not she asked me what was wrong when she noticed my depression at the tender age of around 6. She said she thought I just didn't love her. I asked her if she questioned me about my moods and actions. She said no. I couldn't understand that. Was she afraid of the answer? So afraid that she couldn't ask her own little daughter? In my heart I know that she didn't want to know. Maybe she just couldn't deal with it. But I still deserved better. You would think that any parent would die to protect their child. Not so.

I was so upset up that I had to call my doctor, even at the age of 30. I couldn't focus. I couldn't stop crying. My insecurity will be the death of me. I get so engrossed in the feeling that I'm nothing, that I can't fathom anyone else even caring about me. I need too much reassurance. I think this suffocates people and I can't make anyone happy.

I'm reading a very good book about codependency. I see myself everywhere in it.

I must detach. You don't have to become obsessed in order to love. I need to care for myself. But that's hard to do when you feel worthless about yourself, but empathetic regarding others. How can a person be so detached and still love with the same capacity? If you can't detach, does it cause hatred and/or resentment eventually?

I had a customer who died at my desk. I'd known him since I was 17. I did CPR on him when I was around 35. Everyone else working there just froze. I yelled for help. Two strangers in the office at the time helped me get him out of the chair and onto the floor so I could get started. I did the breathing and compressions. It didn't work. It was a brain aneurism rather than a heart attack. The two strangers disappeared. I never saw them again. Were they angels?

My cousin and I were in an accident. There were four people in her car. It was a two door. After the crash I ended up outside of the car somehow. I was in the back seat and all the windows were up. Very strange feeling. A man dressed all in black came and asked me if we were ok. My cousin had seen him, too. I told him I thought so. I turned around and he was gone. Another angel?

I only wrote about four boyfriends, because they were the only other really significant relationships I've been in besides my marriages. There have been approximately 100 guys I dated or just hooked up with. And I've been proposed to over a dozen times. I would go out every weekend and pick up someone for my sexual pleasure. It's really embarrassing when I look back at how I was living my life...

I have distortive thinking. I can make myself sick just by thinking:

He hasn't called me today. Maybe he doesn't want to talk to me. (Maybe he's just busy).

He's not in a good mood. Maybe I did something wrong. (Maybe he's just having a bad day at work).

He's being very quiet. Maybe I'm suffocating him. (Maybe he's just tired.) *He seems distant. He must not want me anymore.* (Maybe, etc.)

I need to rethink my life and lack of trust in people. I've got to straighten my mind up.

The Wall

There's a wall too high to climb
Built around my heart
But somehow you got by
Through a weakened part

It took just long enough
For me to forget the pain
Then it started over
Now it won't happen again

I really knew better
Than to open up to you
But you made me feel special
And too good to lose

You touched my heart
And I let my hopes rise
Then you walked away
And I watched as they died

How could you be so kind
Then just leave like you did
When you knew how I'd be hurt
After all the time I hid
Now there's a <u>stronger</u> wall too high to climb
Built around my heart

I'll Know

I know when I find him
It will be ecstasy
In my heart, my mind, and soul
I'll know he loves me

And I'll love him
It will be both ways
We'll try to keep each other happy
Throughout each night and day

We'll have such happy lives together
And the Lord my God above
Will give us a glimpse of Heaven
Through this wonderful thing called love

Real Love

I tried so hard when we met
To keep my feelings hidden inside
I didn't want to get my hopes built up
Just to have them pushed aside

Love has never seemed to last for me
Walking away is what people do
And I don't want to feel any more pain
That life can put you through

But you caught my eye and smiled at me
Held out your hand and you said sweetly
Be my lady – walk by my side
Be my best friend – our love won't die

Now you walk by my side every day
You're my closest friend in every way
I live for the moments when I look in your eyes
And see reflections of your love inside

The Sun In My Sky

When I'm with you
Time has no end
And when I'm away
I feel I've lost a friend

You're taking off the chains
Of my long loneliness
And changing all the fears
To shades of happiness

I don't want to be a fool
And lose at love again
So I hide my feelings
And hope someday I'll win

You're the hope in my dreams
The light in my eyes
The answer to my prayers
And the sun in my sky

Yes – you're the sun in my sky

Chapter 15

Pharmacy

I went to the pharmacy to pick up some meds. The waiting area was very crowded. I had turned in my prescription. The pharmacy's assistant had a question for me. Instead of calling me up to the counter, she yelled across the waiting area for me by name. I thought she was calling me up to the counter. But she kept talking and hollered, "Are you a patient at our Mental Health Clinic?". I could have crawled under a chair. It was completely inappropriate. I just sat there and didn't look at anyone – humiliation!

To make things worse, my car was having a problem and would sometimes just die while I was driving. It was very dangerous and scary. Well, it happened to die as I was trying to exit the hospital on to the main street. My car died right at the stop sign. Well, as soon as that happened, everyone was lining up behind me. They didn't know that my car couldn't go and they couldn't see me trying to wave them around. They were all expecting me to pull out and starting to honk. So I got out of the car and waved them around.

When they were all gone, I put my car in neutral and thought I could push it back so people wouldn't think I was just sitting there. I didn't realize there was a slight decline and was outside the car trying to push it. Well, the decline in the drive got the better of me. My car started rolling backwards faster than I could stop it.

To top that off, I had on a dress and heels because I was coming from work. I looked around and there was a truck coming toward me. I knew I had to stop the car NOW. I started running in my heels trying to get into the car. When I got as close as I was able to, I jumped from the long driveway into my car. I slammed into the floorboard and tried to press on the brakes with my hand. The car slowed slightly, but not enough. I took my other hand and shoved the car into park (which I'm sure was not good for the car). But it got the car stopped.

As I was getting up from the floorboard, I noticed some employees out having a smoke break. They, and others in the lot, saw what had happened. No one made any attempt to help me or ask if I was OK. That made me even more embarrassed. I still had my car in park and in my flustered state I put on my sunglasses and hunched down in the front seat until I could compose myself. One man who was driving by, stopped to ask if he could drive me home. Here I was with my mental health issues and broken car issue. I still was shaken up and here comes a man who doesn't offer to look at my car, but would like to pick me up and drive me home. Ugh... I finally got the car started and got home. I traded the car in as soon as I could. And the entire right side of my body's bruising eventually faded...

Chapter 16

Dad's Death

Dad's death was expected, but you still feel the jolt of realization when the end comes. Several times my brother and I were told he wouldn't make it through the night. So we got there as soon as possible. But it's a long flight.

The last time they called, I didn't go. I couldn't afford to keep going. Missing too much work and the cost to get there had drained my finances.

When my brother went the last time, I was told he stood up and just leaned on my brother. I think he was ready to go and needed his only son to get there to take care of the family.

I was at work when the first call came. My brother had promised to keep me up to date on circumstances. He passed away. Then he'd call me back with the news that he'd been shocked back. It seemed that he called me about six times, but I was in a daze by then.

Then the doctors and chaplain told my mother she should let him go. It was at the point that he would be too sick if he did live. So she let him go. I was still in a daze and decided to finish my day at work and not leave. My aunt called and was going to come get me so I just left after that and went home. My third husband drove our little family to the funeral.

When I thought about it later, I decided he didn't deserve my presence there when he passed after all he had done to me. So I felt justified in my mind that it worked out that way due to karma or something to that nature.

Two of the five brothers, my cousins, who had tormented me for so long were pall bearers. I faced them the best I could and acted like nothing ever happened. (Inside I felt horrific terror. But I kept telling myself that they would be gone soon and I wouldn't have to be around them anymore.)

My aunt was supposed to get a family heirloom, my grandfather's organ. But when we were there, he told me he wanted me to have it because he knew I would use it (possibly partially due to his shame). So my mother brought it to my home following his death and due to the fact that my aunt had made no arrangement to go retrieve it. The family had a hay day after that. It was horrible. Eventually I couldn't stand to see it every day. I called my aunt and told if she still wanted it to come get it before I chopped it up for firewood. She got it at last. And I took all the pictures of my father down and put them away. It was a type of cleansing I guess. Don't forget forgiveness...

Chapter 17

Boyfriend #1 - Troy

(Only including long term boyfriends/relationships.)

My sister wanted to introduce me to her boss. I was still married to Troy but met them for lunch on his birthday, or she thought it was. It turned out not to be his birthday. So we just all three had lunch.

He was looking for a place to live, going through a separation at the same time I was and I had a lot of space in the house and could use the rental income. So I let him move in to rent the basement.

Eventually Troy and I became closer and started an intimate relationship. It was evidently more emotional to me and physical to him.

It was like a roller coaster - in love one day – and not the next. He has three beautiful daughters. They have their mother's beauty (Finish) and their father's coloring (Hispanic) – absolutely gorgeous.

We were together for almost five years. I got closer to the girls, and his granddaughter called me Nana. I loved her so much. We separated slowly and he started seeing someone he worked with. Of course, then he moved out. But we were still seeing each other sporadically.

When I found out Troy was very serious about this other woman, I got my son to help me load up everything he had left at my house. I drove to his home. He wasn't there so we unloaded all his belongings in the front yard.

He ended up marrying the other woman. He was her 5th husband. They ended up getting a divorce.

Now Troy's remarried again and I pray for their happiness.

Chapter 18

Dentist

I've had some serious dental work in my life.

I had the same dentist for about 15 years. He knew I was nervous about dental work. He was in the process of doing a root canal. The pain was horrendous on a Friday, when the office was closed. I called his emergency phone number left on his recorder. He told me to meet him at his office right away and he would come in and take a look at my tooth. I was very thankful that he would help me with my pain.

I have tremors and was shaking from that and worse because of the nervous dentist thing.

He gave me two full shots of Novocain, which makes me even shakier. He said he had taken some reflexology classes and could help the shakes if I let him show me some of what he had learned, just on my feet. I said OK. I was in a skirt and heels. He took off my shoes and began to push pressure points. The next thing I knew he had rubbed his hands up my skirt and was trying to fondle me. I got out of the chair and he blocked my exit. He put his arms around me and started to french kiss me. I jerked away from him and got around his body. As I was rushing from his office, I heard him calling out for me to come back. H*** no. I got in my car and headed back to work. When I got there, a friend just looked at me and asked me what was wrong. I started to cry and told her what happened. She told me I had to call the police. I called the police and they had a detective come to the bank and interview me. Of course I was still in shock and crying. My boyfriend and his boss (a friend) came to get me and take me to the police department. They were a very intimidated looking pair. Both are about 6'4" and weighed about 250 - 300 pounds. I signed the report and went back to work.

The detective called and asked me how many men worked in the office. I told him just the dentist. He said he called there and a man answered. When he identified himself as a detective, the man hung up. He immediately drove to the office (maybe five minutes away) and talked to him. He was charging him with felony sexual abuse and harassment (the dentist had tried to call me numerous times – over several days).

The next week his attorney's assistant called me for a phone interview. I told her to go ahead. After she asked me if I gave him permission to remove my shoes, I told her about his reflexology, I said OK. Then I got really mad and told her I DID NOT give him permission to stick his tongue down my throat. She ended the discussion abruptly.

I pressed charges. He wanted to go to court. I worked with an attorney through the courts. He didn't want to settle out of court. The closer we got to the court date, the more the dentist re-considered his decision. The date I went to the court to finalize my pre-case trial, he had a last minute change of heart, and we settled out of court with several stipulations. He was on probation for 2 years, had to take specific counseling classes, had to perform a specified number of hours for free dental work for the elderly, he couldn't work on any female patient without a female employee in attendance for two years, and had to compensate me financially (very little). He was married with a child around the age of two. I wondered if he caused himself a divorce, too…

My root canal had never been completed. So I went to another dentist. When a male assistant walked behind me and touched my shoulder as saying hello, I almost jumped out of my skin.

He accidently broke the tip of a file in my lower jaw. It got infected and I had to go to a specialist to be treated, at their expense. They got the infection cleaned out but never could get the little file tip out. But it hasn't bothered me since.

Now it's been long enough that I can go to my current dentist any time without putting the fear of God in me. Also, now I have dentures, so I hardly ever have to go now anyway.

Chapter 19

My Revelation

It's 3:24 am and I just had a revelation. Bottom line – I've been hiding. Not just recently, but all my life. I've been so afraid that someone would really get to know me that I hid. You know, chances are that if someone gets to know the real you, they may not really like what they see. These feelings can only be the result of extremely low self-esteem, caused by my childhood trauma.

Most parents (I think) try to teach their children to be strong, self-confident individuals who believe in themselves, which would alleviate the low self-esteem issue.

When I was a child, I tried to hide from everything and everyone. That was the beginning. All the attention I got was so negative that I didn't want any. I hid behind my plain clothes and long, straight hair, hanging in my face. I even physically hid in bushes and in my dark closet, away from the pain of the world. I hid my personality and my soul.

I realize now that, as I matured into an adult, I continued down the same path. I hid behind mean men. No personality needed. I thought they would protect me. When I was heavier, I hid behind baggy clothes. As I got thinner, I wore tighter clothes. Yes, this was also a revelation. If people only see the outer shell, maybe they won't see my inner soul (which was mutilated). I have also hidden behind makeup in the past. Personal preference aside, too much attention drawn to the face may also allow hiding of the human element beneath. I felt so unworthy that I thought I was making myself more presentable and acceptable to the "real world", because otherwise I was ugly to myself. It never occurred to me that, perhaps, underneath all of my masks was a sincerely beautiful person. True beauty does, after all, emanate from the soul.

It was disheartening to hear from a close male friend, that men may be viewed me as a sexual object, not noticing the real me. However, that's when I realized that maybe – just maybe - the real me could be worth knowing.

Following all of the above self-analysis, I must conclude that no one knows the real me, including myself. This leaves me with the mission of finding my hidden self and releasing it to the world, with dreams of self-evolution.

The hardest part in bringing out the real me is by trying to remove the masks layer by layer. If my heart is left open to the world, I will be very vulnerable; which usually leads to pain in my case. The thought of bearing myself to others can also strengthen my fear of rejection and abandonment, at least until the faith in myself has grown to some degree. Telling others my deepest feelings could possibly drive them away or repel them in some way. However, I suppose one must take chances and have faith in the goodness of humanity.

It's hard for me to believe that I've never been able to choose what I want to do. I have always let others make the decisions because I was unsure of their faith in my decisions. I believe it's time in my life for me to help decide certain issues, if not make the entire decision alone. However, at this point, being alone, the decisions will have to be my own anyway.

One part of me always believed that a big, strong, loving man would come along, take me by the hand, and lead me out in the world, into a reality I have never known. Show me how to love, live, and laugh. Take me places and show me the real things in life that count. I sometimes wonder at myself for having such Cinderella hopes (the fairy tale does not exist). However, as I think back to my childhood, the dreams or fairy tales may have been one of the things that kept me going through all of the hard times. I hate to admit it but, though weak, the dream still exists at some level.

Realistically, my spirituality is what pulled me through. I started going to church regularly when I was around 15. I knew I was never really alone, that I had Him to talk to and lean on. Even when it seemed that I was really completely alone, I knew that He held me and wept with me, which left me with a hope beyond imagination for a life worth living.

Singing with the church opened me up to doing drama in school. I also went to State, some of the best times I remember in my entire life, and received one ratings and medals. I was in plays, a musical, and a member of choir and swing choir. I went to a local college to audition for music and singing. I got a $5,000 grant – but at this point, I already left and was living with my 1st husband, didn't go – BAD TIMING AND BAD DECISION.

The Wall

There's a wall too high to climb
Built around my heart
But somehow you got by
Through a weakened part

It took just long enough
For me to forget the pain
Then it started over
Now it won't happen again

I really knew better
Than to open up to you
But you made me feel special
And too good to lose

You touched my heart
And I let my hopes rise
Then you walked away
And I watched as they died

How could you be so kind
Then just leave like you did
When you knew how I'd be hurt
After all the time I hid

Now there's a <u>stronger</u> wall too high to climb
Built around my heart

The Past

It was long ago in another place
When you first seemed special to me
But that was in another world
And it was never meant to be

When I saw you again
We talked for a while
We spoke of old things
That made us both smile

You're a man in every way
Very caring and kind
And in a world like this today
That's so very hard to find

I put my arm through yours
And you walked by my side
You told me of your life
And asked me of mine

Now we're back in separate worlds
So far apart again
But I'll always think of you
As a very special friend

You showed me the world
On a cool summer night
Then held me in your arms
Til almost morning light

Chapter 20

On-Line Dating

Now, this is a joke. I thought it would work, but no.

1) A mortician. He wanted a pretty girl on his arm. Very much older. Nah.
2) This one said he was handsome and a professional. I met him for drinks. Lordy no. Very nerdy looking with his glasses sliding down continuously. Couldn't look me in the eyes and was a professional janitor. Nah
3) 19 years old. Had a drink and let it go.
4) A widower with a daughter. Reminded me of Sleepless in Seattle. Talked on the phone. Baby 3 months old. Wife passed and in-laws were fighting for custody. I asked why. He said he had been in prison. I asked what for. Bank robbery. I worked in banking for 25 years. Freaked me out. NO WAY.
5) Met at a safe place. Went to downtown for a drink. Told me his ex was messing with a biker gang and drugs. They were after him. They had driven by his van while parked. They shot all across the side. And here he had me at an outside café. I told him it was time to go. What if they were following him and drove past us and started shooting. NAH.

I stopped doing that. On to the rest of my life.

Chapter 21

Boyfriend #2 - Beau

I sent him a copy of a poem I wrote. It was 'Strawberry Rose'. It was beautiful to me but was only a dream we once shared. It was an emotional time for me.

I understood Beau sometimes felt frustration by the way I express myself. When I'm hurt, usually I use sarcasm as my shield. That's the only way I know how to react for protection.

I miss the way he wrote stories to me and sent me flowers for no reason. (And it was funny getting barked at my job – by a man.) I never got angry with him. When he got angry, he would withdraw from people. In spite of all that, I loved him for the person he was and the goodness in his heart.

The point is that we all have our strengths and weaknesses. However, love accepts the good and bad – as I accepted his. If Beau couldn't accept me for whom I am, then I must respect his opinion and feelings. As he said, it is what it is.

You said if we were ever apart, you would come and get me. You told me that you are my love song. Never stop the dance. You couldn't imagine anyone else with me. You even serenaded me from outside my window.

I told Beau once that I'm an ALL or NOTHING kind of person. I have trouble with the – do I belong or do I NOT belong – feeling. I needed to be accepted for who I am, just as he did. And I needed to know that I would be loved through good times and bad times. Love knows no boundaries.

When I'm hurt, I start to re-build the emotional wall around myself for protection. Like he said – love hurt is the worst kind of hurt. But I love the way you made me laugh.

I have a wonderful friend who says, 'they just done crawled on up in there'. I can relate. He's helped me to see another side of myself and realize that it's OK to completely let go now. First – I lived it for years. Second - I relived it for years. And third – I can finally let go and be proud of who I have become in spite of my experiences.

It's all in how you play the hand you're dealt. Some are dealt a winning hand. Others get lucky later in life. Still others have to bluff their way through life. And there are the flat-out losers. I guess I'd rather start at the bottom of life and work my way up. I want to know and understand everything happening each and every step of the way. (No rose-colored glasses for me.)

It amazes me to sometimes meet people who honestly think that life is a bowl of cherries! But wonder of wonders, they do exist. Have they never known pain or were they just better at dealing with it? Maybe some are emotionally weak people whom God spared from too many horrors, knowing that they couldn't deal with it. If that were the case, I hope God would be proud of me for the strength I have shown. Amen.

I've been speaking with Beau recently. Who knew where that would go. He ended up marrying someone else. Now they are divorced and we're still friends and talk once in a while.

I'm seeing someone else now sporadically. If my relationship doesn't work out, he wants another chance with me. Now he met a new girl – who knows what will happen… I wish them the most happiness.

They didn't get married. His father, a very good man, had died in the home. She was continuously sick and said it was his dead father causing it. I loved his dad. He wouldn't scare a woman. He loved them too much. He's alone again. And we're talking again. And he's got a new woman in his life. BE HAPPY.

Strawberry Rose

I was never going to let myself love again
Not let anyone in who could cause me pain
I pushed away all those who wanted to be near
And swore I would never cry another tear

I always acted like I was open and free
Not letting anyone know the real me
I buried my identity deep within
To keep myself from ever hurting

Then you crept into my life and soul
You took my heart in your hand and held it so close
You whispered sweet words of love in my ear
And melted every single doubt and fear

You make love to me in so many ways
Showing me brilliance in every day
You let me know that you're my love song
And that our love will always remain strong

I'm your dream woman, fly girl, and helper to your son
I know now and always you're my only one
The love we share is deep and no one knows
We shared a sunset, a moonrise, and a strawberry rose

Another Try

You came along and swept me off my feet
Best looking man I've ever seen
You took me by the hand
Said you'd be my loving man
And show me how life should really be

Too much of my past kept me feeling blue
But it never seemed to even bother you
No you didn't care about my past
Cause you knew you'd be my last
No man before could hold a candle to you

Neither of us wanted to try love anymore
Because we'd both been hurt badly before
But we gave this love a chance
I never knew so much romance

Now we'll never have to wonder about love anymore
I've been lost for such a long time
I didn't really think I would ever find
A man who'd love me and always be mine

Chapter 22

Boyfriend #3 - Randy

Now this was a fun upbeat kind of guy. We rode to Sturgis every year we were together. Randy was a biker and a drinker – had a fridge in the garage with a spigot on it, always full of beer. He also smoked weed and was a dealer. He had lots of friends and his life was one big party.

This was around the time I had a bad time with colitis. I lost so much weight that I was wearing a size one in jeans. I started passing out and couldn't party so much anymore. He lost interest. (Who wouldn't?)

Randy started dating another girl I knew back then. She went through rehab and couldn't be around him anymore with the alcohol and drugs.

So he was off to another playground and is living with someone else now. He had a bad motorcycle accident and is lucky to be alive.

Randy does work on motorcycles and cars now at his own shop in a city just next to where I live.

He's doing well and I wish him the best. Remember forgiveness.

**

Somewhere around this time, I lost the most beautiful aunt in the world. May she rest in peace as she cares for her awesome son.

Chapter 23

Husband #4 - Kyle

I met Kyle through Randy. We lived together for a while and then got married eventually. We seemed perfect for each other. We were both homebodies and wrapped our lives together out of love.

We rode our Harley all the time and just had fun.

Kyle's middle daughter and four children moved here from out of state and lived with us for several years. She brought a friend along. They had it out and she took her back home and then came back to us. I loved being Nana. And my mom loved being Great Nana.

But his daughter was a lazy person who didn't take care of her living space or children. She met lots of men and flaunted herself to all men. She was extremely overweight which made her breasts larger, too. And she wanted everyone to see them. Open to the world.

We usually got along really well. Just some spats once in a while. Then my son moved back from college and stayed here with his girlfriend.

Then my husband's youngest daughter moved here with her one child. She was only here for several months.

Our house was <u>full</u> of people and we never had a dull moment. Kyle was an alcoholic. But he hardly drank at all when we were together. And his daughters and their children eventually moved out. The middle daughter got married and the younger one moved back to be with her mom. At one time, we had 11 people living here.

At my husband's job, they had him update his annual forms. He said he thought he was filling out a form for insurance but it was really for a Flexible Spending Account. They started withholding a lot of money from his paycheck. They told him the only way to change it (per IRS rules) was to have a family status change. Therefore, we got divorced but stayed together. His paychecks were normal again but I think that's when our relationship started going downhill fast.

One day Kyle was upset at me about who knows what. I obviously keep living from my past distortive thinking. I know how to push buttons. I think I just wanted someone who could see through my pain and still love me. He left work after a half day and went to the bar. (We used to have so much fun in there.) He told me later he had drunk 10-12 scotches – no water, no ice. He was totally drunk. I got ahold of his keys and took off the one for the motorcycle and house. He was getting violent and threatening more physical abuse. My son's girlfriend called 911. She told them he was big and asked them to send a lot of cops. They did. The police called the photographer to come to the house and take pictures of the bruises he left on my arms. They arrested him for domestic abuse. I called his daughter and let her know, so she could bail him out. In the meantime, he thought no one would know where he was. Therefore, he called his employer and asked if they would bail him out. They told him no and that was the end of that job.

It turned out that Kyle had been planning to move to his brother's down in the southern part of the state for at least the last year. He had told my mom's husband he was leaving me around a year before this occurred. Who knew?

He moved to his brothers finally and eventually they got tired of him being there and kicked him out.

He moved to a small apartment in the city that his middle daughter was living in. Kyle would watch his grandkids on the weekends. He couldn't handle them all at once, and had one come over each weekend rotating them.

One day, his youngest granddaughter was at school on the playground. A teacher overheard her tell another child that her Grandpa loved her best and let her suck his weenie. The school immediately called in Social Services/Child Protection. They got all the children and their mother and started questioning them. Turns out that he was having the little girls undress and was taking close up pictures of their private parts. Then he would copy the photos to his computer.

The police immediately arrested Kyle and confiscated his cell phone and computer. He admitted to taking the photos but denied molesting them. The girls told a different story. It turned out that was all true. He also had a lot of pictures on his computer that were also other children's (and some adults) private parts.

He admitted to me also that he took pictures of the granddaughters but didn't do anything else. He also told me that he had a new 'hobby' of collecting pictures of vaginas. Many were shaved and it couldn't be determined if they were underage or not. I think the charges against him were more extreme with underage children.

I was served with a summons to appear. My mom and I drove to the courthouse. They ended up not needing my testimony. We stayed for the court session that day since we were already there.

Evidently the two older granddaughters had already testified. The youngest would be asked questions, and turn to look at her grandpa and clammed up. Therefore, they allowed a taping of the interview of the youngest granddaughter's testimony. She was shy at first, obviously. The person interviewing her gained her trust and she told what happened to her. It was horrible. She said after the photos he would touch her and wanted her to touch him. He even told her that the white 'stuff' on the end of his penis was good. He had her put her finger in it and taste how good it was. She said it tasted like snot. This was a six year old granddaughter. Lord God in Heaven – what was he thinking/doing??!!!

Kyle was charged with 75 charges, including, but not limited to, child abuse, child pornography, child sexual molestation, abusing his position of authority, etc. He was found guilty of 71 of the charges and was sentenced to 150 years in prison. He's eligible for parole in 2034 or so, in his 80's.

I have been in communication with him, maybe just for closure - I'm not really sure.

He called me about two months ago. He was crying profusely. He had suffered a stroke a week prior. How pitiful and horrific this entire ordeal was and is. He's currently going through rehab and is improving a bit.

I pray for the grandchildren and ask God to heal them from the horrors they went through and will go through the rest of their lives. I know the pain and insecurities they will live through and I hope they have God in their hearts to help them through their lives.

As an afterthought, I'm so very glad Kyle and I were divorced before these atrocious situations took place. It makes me wonder if he had prior similar incidents. Who really knows.

Four Time Loser

When you're a four time loser
And on the fifth strike you're out
You build a wall too high to climb
Made of insecurity, fear, and doubt

Honesty is long since gone
And openness a lie
Then you start to really wonder
If it helps to even try

Then someone might come along
Who's open, true, and kind
But it's hard to even think about
With the fears that rule your mind

Life's a long, hard road to walk alone
And it seems like all you can do
But it's a shame to miss out on something special
From what fear of pain has done to you

If no one learns from me
Or profits from my being
Will there be any reason
For me ever living

Chapter 24

Psychiatric Hospital

I've been admitted to the Psychiatric Hospital four times (lock down) for suicidal and/or homicidal thoughts and/or tendencies, depression, and medication regulation. Once you're in there they have to keep you at least 72 hours. They try to teach you ways to handle your emotions and life issues the best they can. And they try to regulate your medications. I'm not so sure that they do any good. One time I was in, I was on the phone and a male patient in there for no obvious reason, walked over to me and screamed at me to get off the f*****g phone. I yelled back at him that I would get off the f*****g phone when I was done. He didn't bother me anymore.

However, he also body slammed a female patient who was pregnant with twins and caused her to miscarry both babies. He was really locked down – 24 hour watch.

I feel so all alone among all these other patients. Lucky for me, my mother came to visit me all the time. Also, my sister came up from out of state to help my mom and to visit me. I sit alone in the dayroom wishing my son would visit me. He's all I really have. He and my grandson are my legacy. But I know he doesn't have enough gas to drive this far, so I don't blame him. I've been in the hospital for a month now. I feel agony in my soul to not see him for so long. I love him so much.

One of my cats had pancreatic cancer. Mom told me her husband's friend took him to be put down while I was still hospitalized. They waited three days to tell me, worried about my reaction. I sobbed. Not even a chance to say goodbye.

I didn't have an income that would allow me to pay for surgery. I had just lost 25 years in banking. I had worked my way up to $50,000 a year and Social Security Disability dropped me down to approximately $20,000.

I just feel sorrow and pain. I smile at the world and pretend to be happy – to make others happy. But I'm crying inside. My veins are filled with acid as my heart hardens. I know it will get better some day. Just a waiting game.

Oh, wait. It's 2nd visitation. They called my name. My heart skips a beat. Maybe it's my son. But when I got to the visiting room, no one is there for me. Turns out the visitors were for a patient with the same name in adolescents not for adults. My heart plummeted to the bottom of my stomach like a lead weight and I cried all the way back to the unit. I'm sure my son didn't want to come around a psych hospital visiting his mom and seeing all the other patients that were off in the head.

When my son hurts me, the blood in my veins turns to acid. My heart nearly stops as I try to understand what I did wrong and caused him to love/hate me so much. I love my son very much and throughout all of our hard times together, I know he loves me, too. Also, I will never stop loving him. I've just got to learn tough love. It's a little late in the game but still needs to be done. Better late than never?

Chapter 25

Step-Dad

Mom came to visit me and support me as much as she could. They referred me to a Reach Program – step down program. The next day I went through their intake process and was immediately placed in their halfway house. It housed 12 people at a time, half men and half women.

I have good insurance with medicare and supplemental coverage with another insurance company. However, they don't accept my insurance, so they signed me in as Indigent.

I'm taking about 30 pills a day. It's very hard to manage them. Sometimes I get them mixed up. Sometimes my whole life feels mixed up still. My mom helped me sort my pills until I was able to do it myself.

My step-dad came with mom to take me to the halfway house. He informed me that I was a burden to him and was coming between his and my mother's marriage. I, at the age of late 40s, had been admitted to the psych hospital 4 times. I was in tears the entire ride. I was losing my mind. My mom was yelling back at him. I told him that's why nobody in the family liked him. He is so mean! He clapped his hands really hard and was acting sarcastic. Then just as mom and I were done with the intake processing, he texted her to take the RTD bus home and left her. I texted him he wasn't much of a man and maybe my husband #4 wasn't so bad after all. About ten minutes later he called her and said he'd be right back to pick her up. What a jerk he was. I will never trust him for anything. Thinking back I don't think I ever have. He just did things for me because of mom or to earn my trust. I have to admit it was gracious of him to have my garage door fixed without being asked. But I'm just so tired of him being rude and nasty. He was so disgusting. It doesn't make any sense why my mother had told him about my past in detail. He would repeat things that she told him, which he in turn held against me and threw in my face. My mother also helped catch my bills up since I wasn't there. She has redone her area of the houses, putting in a lot of funds herself.

He yelled at me about how I am. It's not something I asked for. And no one protected me from his verbal abuse. He also told me once that when I did cut my arm I should cut a little deeper and end it all for once. What a b*****d.

My step-dad tried to push my mom out of her vehicle in front of two of Kyle's grandkids, my step-grandkids. (He was driving but they were at a stop.) One was in shock and the other was bawling her little eyes out as she told us what happened. He also got mad at my mother and shoved her behind a door so hard that her body went through the wall in their house.

I can't deal with him anymore. I wish my mom had married a nicer man. She seemed to also be drawn to mean men as my sister and I were. Looking in the wrong places?

Some people are here to teach us something about ourselves. Sometimes they're only in our lives for a short while and others are life-long. But the lessons will last hopefully. I only saw a good side of him several times during their relationship. If people could only tell what their relationships would like in advance, it would have saved a lot of emotional pain in the long run.

The damage to my mother was done. My mom came to live with me. She's been here for four years and in the process they had a messy divorce. But my mom is taken care of financially. At least that worked out. She's having issues being without a companion. I know what that's like. It's so hard. And I hate seeing her depressed and crying. God will care for her.

Later, several months ago, my mom got a call from the coroner's office. They found my stepdad deceased in his home. The mailman saw the mail stacking up more and more. He finally called the police. They came to the house and found him. He had been deceased approximately three to four weeks. Mom and I went over to see if everything was going smoothly. His daughter and her husband were there to make sure the house was locked up. Mom still had a key. She opened the door and the odor almost knocked us all over. It was horrific.

Biohazard clean-up was needed before anyone could go in to handle his possessions. His daughter had a copy of the will and will get us a copy. It looks like the estate will be handled and whatever's left, since their divorce was final in September, will be split between his two biological children.

My mom will need to file against the estate for her portion of his Retirement, Social Security, Maintenance, etc… Hopefully she turns out very well in the outcome. My stepdad's daughter told my mom to take what she wanted. We went over and went through the garage. My mother lost her step and broke her femur. My stepdad's son wanted some of the items back. He came and got what he wanted and all was well.

Chapter 26

Son

I don't even know where to start about my son. He's like a light in my soul. At age 25, I was waiting to go in to labor, my mom came to help me out. We went to a large church that we seldom attended. There was a guest speaker. He was really preaching an intense sermon. All of a sudden, he swirled around and stared me straight in the eyes. I felt like a bolt of lightning stabbed through me. My baby kicked like a solid punch at the same exact time. My mom said he was blessed in my womb.

When he was a little guy (about 4), he helped me pass out all his used toys to the children who lived in our apartment complex (low income families). One of the mothers said her kids had no toys at all. My son has such a beautiful soul. I was working for minimum wage at the bank and considered low income. I was accepted into the housing program but made too much money to qualify for food stamps.

I had a pearl ring. The pearl fell out and I never found it. I cried and he (still around 4 years old) hugged me so tight and begged his mommy not to cry.

His class in elementary school went downtown. When he came home he told me he worried I'd be mad at him because he gave his field trip spending money to a man sitting by the street who looked really hungry. How can you pass up that bundle of love, my son.

I felt so proud of him that day. I hugged him and loved on him.

One day we watched an old black and white movie. A man in the movie dreamed of being a musical conductor. He got the chance to do so but didn't have a jacket. The one they let him use was too tight. When he raised his arms, the jacket sleeves ripped. The audience was laughing at him and he just sat down and cried. My son cried with him and asked me how those people could be so mean.

When he was a little older (10), he made me a candle light dinner, I came home and he came out to the garage. He made me close my eyes and walked me to the kitchen. The lights were out except for two candles on the table. He had made macaroni and cheese, fish sticks, and salad. How precious is that?

You can see the beauty of my son, and I love him with all my heart. I lost three babies and got to keep him. Thank you God!

It's hard to realize when my son went from such a loving child to being so harsh with people, probably at a later time, when I divorced his adopted dad. He can also be the darkest part of me. He rebelled horribly.

Currently I have gone through so much drama with him that I had to give him totally back to God. He has taken advantage of my love in many ways.

I hope everything straightens out with him. I still see him as my precious baby. Time for tough love.

I ended up telling him to move out. He has a girlfriend and moved in with her. It didn't work out so well and after several months I let him come home. He started a new job and is saving up to move back out. (But sometimes they get along for a while.) I told him he had to move out again in a few months. He's now working two jobs and trying to save. They live together currently. They have disagreements, as we all sometimes do, but somehow keep coming out on top. I think they make a good couple. She keeps him on his toes.

SON

Baby it's you
That brightens my day
Without you around
Who'd show me the way

When everything I do
Seems to go wrong
Your love cheers me up
And makes me feel strong

You put your little arms
Around my neck – oh so tight
That the clouds go away
And things are alright

You smile up at me
With your small shining face
And the problems I have
Seem to slip in to place

Chapter 27

Boyfriend #4 - Sean

I had a plumbing problem and called a man for help (referred by my Church). After we met, we started seeing each other. It's been about three and a half years now. He treats me like no one else ever has and he's so attentive.

We've only had two disagreements since we met. Sean yelled so loud, it was like bellowing, telling me to get the f*** out of his house. If that happens again, I don't know how I'll react. Just leave I guess.

Valentine's Day 2013, he sent me a dozen roses, gave me chocolates, and took me to dinner. We double dated with his son and his girlfriend. I really do love him and he's very kind to everyone.

He broke up with me for about six months. Now he's as sweet as can be. During the meantime, I was writing on a computer dating line. I met a guy. We started dating on line. When my boyfriend wanted me back, I had to make a choice. I explained it to Danny, my online friend. He was very upset because he wasn't the one I chose and called me the worst names you can think of.

Sean's a wonderful man and is very understanding. And he loves me in spite of all my past. But they all say that at the beginning. Then, if they get mad, they throw it in your face. We ended our relationship when we determined that he didn't have enough time in his life for me. Single dad, teenage son, working nights, trying to balance the home life. It just wouldn't work.

Sean and I are broken up again. He has no time for me. I broke it off this time. Still friends.

Now he wants me back. The other guy and my dating threw him for a loop.

I'm staying with Sean. We've made up and our relationship is flourishing.

NEVER MIND !!

Unsure

The fears of a lifetime
Were set deep inside
But you came on so slowly
I couldn't even hide

You showed me some kindness
By just being a friend
And I felt at that moment
That my heart just might mend

You said you were lonely
When we met the next time
And you wanted to see me
If I didn't mind

Just don't break my heart
And I'll try not to hide
Cause I'm still very fragile
Deep down inside

The first time I saw you
I wanted you to be mine
Cause you seemed so special
And that's so hard to find

You broke down the walls
Round my once broken heart
And gave me what I needed
To have a new start

Chapter 28

My Job

I started working for a bank at an entry position at 18. I flew through advances from within and I was a quick learner.

I worked at that bank for 22 years. And I loved it. They advanced me every chance they got it. What a compliment to me. They offered me new positions as they came up. I learned every hourly job in the bank. Even without a college degree, they still gave me the job advances based on my job history. Up to internal auditing and assistant to the president. Then I did credit analysis work. I changed banks because they were talking about closing our office, which did happen several months later

I was having some personal problems – mentally and physically. Three weeks prior to my dismissal I had been admitted to my first visit to the Psych Hospital. They knew it was for mental issues. My medication was altered and left me my brain foggy. A customer issue came up which was admittedly my error. I mentioned disability to my boss.

The next Friday, our department was going on a team building outing. Around noon, I was called up to the president's office. I asked a friend to wait for me because I was riding with her.

My employment was being terminated. I cried (which I hardly ever do). Their reason in the letter stated that I was no longer able to perform my duties. They said there was a taxi waiting for me outside and to pack my stuff up with supervision. When I went to do so, everyone was gone. How embarrassing.

I thought my life was over. I never kept in touch with anyone, due to extreme anxiety. I didn't press the disability issue with my employer. I filed myself through the state and was approved. I've been on disability on around nine years now. It more than cut my income in half. Now I go to Food Banks monthly.

Chapter 29

Update

My mom has talked me in to renting to several people:

1. *Homeless Psychotic – here for a short time*
2. *Loud, obnoxious – no way - didn't stay*
3. *Homeless – still here*
4. *Homeless & jobless – here one month*

Renter #4 wouldn't follow a rule about parking in the driveway and threatened my life because of that rule. So he told me he was going to cook and put cyanide in my food to kill me. Then he waved a butcher knife at me and with a wicked grin said, "Now will you let me park in drive?" I told him no and the police were called. He was made to move out immediately.

My therapist retired about two years ago and hasn't been replaced. I've been in therapy for about 30 years now. I do, however, still see a Psychiatrist (I'm very comfortable with her!) and Primary Care Physician and take a barrage of medications. I also self-medicate by smoking weed. I do have a medical marijuana license.

Prozac, Abilify, Klonopin, Seroquel, Cogentin, Ambien, Ativan, Gabapentin, Atorvastatin, Levothyroxine, Metformin, Omeprazole, Vicodin, and Aspirin.

A doctor at the Psyhciatric Hospital told me zinc and selenium were to alleviate hair loss from so many medications. Cranberry – I get UTIs (urinary tract infection). Iron was to help strengthen my blood (following a blood transfusion). The aspirin is for my heart.

I also had surgery on my bladder. This caused internal bleeding (grapefruit sized hematoma) and pneumonia. The second surgery was to drain the hematoma. However, the surgeon cut through a mass of blood veins. I almost bled out (died) three times and had to have a blood transfusion. The third surgery was done vaginally and was successful. I figure I should only pay for the first surgery, but it doesn't work that way. I'm lucky and glad to be alive. I get by the best I can. The surgery(s) blocked something and have left me with no libido or orgasms. I told the doctor and he's giving me medicine and wants to see if it works. If not – he's referring me to a sex therapist…

I called an attorney off TV regarding vaginal mesh surgeries due to the problems. I don't know if anything will come of that. Waiting for call back.

Chapter 30

Boyfriend #5 – Danny vs #4 - Sean

When Sean broke up with me, my brother helped me sign up on a dating line. That's when I met Danny. We've been corresponding in writing and by phone since (almost a year starting in 2013). That was when Sean wanted me back. I tried one last time with Sean. That's all over.

Danny planned on coming out to meet me in person and see how it goes. He's sarcastic, witty, and funny and he keeps me laughing. We'll see.

In the meantime, Sean came back into my life again. He wrote me love letters and brought flowers - and he won my heart back. No more Danny. Sean is also very romantic and I love that in him.

I told Danny I was back with Sean. I was cussed out (showing his true colors).

Sean and I are talking about getting married soon. He said every time he heard a love song, he thought about me. We plan on being together the rest of our lives. He makes me feel so good about everything.

NEVER MIND !!

Chapter 31

Dreams & Journals

(DREAMS UNDERLINED AND CAPITALIZED)

In my dreams exists an horrific and ugly world of its own. When I dream, it seems like real life. I feel it, I see it, and I live it. If only I could remember while I'm dreaming that it's not real and force myself to wake up.

I WAS THE MOTHER OF FOUR INNOCENT, IDENTICAL LITTLE GIRLS (LOOKED LIKE MY CHILDHOOD PHOTOS). I MURDERED ALL FOUR. I WAS WANTED BY THE POLICE. I CUT MY HAIR TO DISGUISE MYSELF. I HAD TO RUN, RUN, RUN. ALWAYS HIDING.

I represented my father, the self-hatred he must have felt. The four little girls represented me: innocence, self-esteem, trust, and love. He murdered the child in me.

HE FORCED ME DOWN AND TORE OFF MY CLOTHING. HE WAS ATTEPTING TO KISS ME AND LAUGHING AT MY STRUGGLES TO FREE MYSELF. THE HARDER I TWISTEED, YELLED, AND CRIED – THE MORE HE LAUGHED. IT MUST HAVE BEEN GREAT SPORT FOR HIM.

HE TOUCHED ME EVERYWHERE. HE PENETRATED ME. IT HURT SOOOO BAD. HE ROARED WITH LAUGHTER AND LEERED AT ME WITH A STRANGE LIGHT IN HIS EYES. I FELT DISGUST, HATE, AND OVERWHELMING SHAME. I CRIED AND SCREAMED. I FEEL SUCH LOATHING FOR HIM – THE REVOLTING PERSON WHO THINKS HE'S A MAN. HOW MUCH WORSE COULD HELL BE?

I woke with a start. Just another nightmare. When will it end? Maybe never – I've heard from some.

I have been diagnosed by many Psychiatrists with: Major Depression, Bi-Polar II with Psychotic Features, Chronic Post Traumatic Stress Disorder (PTSD), Schizoaffective, Suicidal Tendencies, Homicidal, Self-Mutilation tendencies (to alleviate internal pain that can't be releaved), Body Memories (feeling the touch that isn't there), Dissociation, Emotional Detachment, Distortive Thinking, Agoraphobia, Diabetes II, Lymphocytic Colitis, Essential Familial Tremors, Left Bundle Branch Block-LBBB (heart issue), panic/anxiety attacks, and hypothyroidism. I also had Bell's Palsy, however, it went away in approximately a month. Doctors have estimated my depression began at around five years of age. Sometimes I use sarcasm to get through the anger and/or pain.

I just can't seem to get his hands off of me. The 'body memories' are sometimes too strong. I may go out of my mind. I can't think. I can't focus. I don't know what to do. My head hurts. I'm shaking, shaking, shaking. I feel like dying. I'm trapped in a state of dazed illusion and I can't get out. One of my therapists suggested that I pretend I'm in a suit of armor and imagine that it cannot be penetrated. It helps somewhat.

This is my life as an incest survivor. Not much of a life – is it? But it's all I've got. How am I supposed to function and concentrate on my job? I can't clear my head of all the horror swimming in it. The lasting affects cloud my mind (or the medication). **I have determined that the way I was raised does affect your actions and thoughts all through your life**.

Does my father know he killed my childhood? How I tried to hide from him? Would he even care if he knew? I sincerely doubt it. Does he understand that he scarred me for life, that my soul had been damaged? I don't think so. Would he care that I can trust no one and I feel worthless? No! If he cared – none of this would have happened.

If he were still alive, what would I do? I guess it doesn't matter since he's not. However, when I'm in some type of aggressive mood, I have dreamed of killing him. So vividly that I felt myself stabbing him in the heart. With the feeling of my closed fist around the end of the hilt hit his chest. It felt so real.

I must remember that he's gone. I have survived and he can't harm me anymore. But for some reason I can't see this when I'm having a nightmare. The fear and disgust could easily consume me if I don't keep a close watch on myself at times like these. And I fear that my lack of trust in people will never leave me.

Of course, I've had to deal with these issues for years. Sometimes when I get in a deep depression, I might talk too much to the wrong person, or perhaps too loudly to the wrong person. You know how gossip travels – lightning fast and twisted.

An employee overheard a remark I made to another employee (trusted) regarding a prescription and 'mental health'. It was repeated and spread.

YOU TRIED TO CHASE ME DOWN. I KEPT RUNNING. YOU STOPPED AND I WASN'T SURE WHAT YOU WERE DOING. I TURNED AROUND. YOU WERE HOLDING MY SON AS AN INFANT AND THREATENING TO THROW HIM IN A BATHTUB FILLED WITH BLEACH, TO BURN HIS SKIN OFF.

The other bank employee on the receiving end of the story seemed extremely concerned about me. And I figured it out. In reality the employee was concerned for her safety and asked my friend if I was going 'postal'. Now isn't that a kick? I guess she feared that I'd go loony and come in shooting. Is this Defamation of Character? I was told that I jump topics like a crazy person. (Just my point.)

Of course my friend helped in her innocent way. Her reply was that I would never do anything like that. Her second line was that if was going to hurt anyone, it would be myself. Now I'm postal and suicidal. I'm really stuck between a rock and a hard place this time. Just wait until some other gossip comes along and my story will disappear. But what a blow to my soul.

I had to tell my boss at this point. I know of employees who have contacted Human Resources with lesser issues. If it were reported that I am a potential danger to work with, I would hate to think of the outcome.

It would be such a different feeling to be able to tell someone absolutely anything about yourself without worrying about future incrimination or personal judgment. I've never had that comfort before. Most people never look at you the same and skitter away when they see you coming. Run.

THE DARK MAN STOOD OUSIDE WAITING FOR ME. ONCE I SAW HIM, IT WAS TOO LATE TO GO BACK IN. NO ONE FOLLOWED ME OUT TO HELP ME. HE WANTED ME. I REFUSED HIM. HE MADE HIS BIG, BLACK DOG ATTACK ME. THEY MERGED INTO ONE BEING – TOP HALF MAN, BOTTOM HALF DOG, ABOUT NINE FEET TALL. HORRID, DISGUSTING. HE RAPED ME MADLY. THERE ARE NO WORDS TO DESCRIBE THE ABOMINATION.

* * * * * * * * * * * * * * *

MY DAD HELD ME DOWN AND TOUCHED ME EVERYWHERE. HE HAD A FRIEND WITH HIM THIS TIME. I CRIED, KICKED, SCREAMED – ALL TO NO AVAIL. HE LAUGHED IN MY FACE AS HE TOOK ME OVER AND OVER. THEY TOOK TURNS – HE AND HIS FRIEND. IT WASN'T JUST FOR A NIGHT. IT LASTED

MONTHS AND MONTHS. THERE WAS ABSOLUTELY NO WAY OUT.

I felt literal disgust, shame, and demoralization. I can still feel the physical pain, even now as I remember the dream. The 'body memories' won't let go.

OH NO! I WAS IN THE SHOWER. I LOOKED AT THE WINDOW. THERE STOOD MY FATHER LEERING AT ME. SOMEONE WAS WITH HIM. THE OTHER PERSON TURNED AWAY IN SHAME AS HE REALIZED WHAT MY FATHER WAS DOING. I SCREAMED AND TRIED TO HIDE MYSELF FROM HIM. THIS IRRITATED HIM TO THE POINT THAT HE WENT INSIDE THE HOUSE TO THE DOOR AND BROKE IT DOWN. HE PHYSICALLY GRABBED ME, TRYING TO FORCE HIMSELF ON ME. THE OTHER PERSON AGAIN TURNED AWAY IN RED-FACED DISGUST. I FELT MORE EMBARASSED THAN I EVER HAD IN MY LIFE. IT WAS BAD ENOUGH TO BE TREATED THIS WAY – BUT TO HAVE OTHERS INVOLVED AND REACT IN THIS MANNER BY DISGUSTED AVOIDANCE SHAMED ME TO NO END.

It seems that the nightmares will never end – but I'm getting better at dealing with them. I told a friend about the dreams and the shame it brings me. Oh, that hurts emotionally to remember. I can feel the physical vaginal pain of the incidents.

A HUGE SPIDER IS TRYING TO ATTACK ME. DAD WATCHES AND LAUGHS.

"I don't blame my mother, but forgive her everything". Quoted from a TV show.

Other TV quotes. "We're not bodies with spiritual beings; we're spiritual beings with bodies." "The finish line is just the beginning of a whole new race." "To lead, you must learn to follow." "Bitterness will drain your love."

DAD DIED. THAT'S OK! UGH - BUT HE IS STILL WATCHING ME. I DON'T KNOW WHERE HE ENDED UP.

I told Husband #4 that I'm obsessed with death when we went to the book store. I looked at books regarding death. I want to cut my wrist, which releases my physical pain. Depression is a very large part of my life.

I'm having a birthday. I'd rather just let it go. I don't like being the center of attention. Please don't look at me!

I'm depressed again. My head tells me that I'm no good. My soul feels like it's been trodden upon. I need pain (cut or burn).

Dear Father God, please make him leave me alone – even after his death he still haunts me…`

Today I feel so unsure of myself. I'll have to watch and see if this is a cycle. One day depression, the next uncertainty. I know I am myself and must learn to control my emotions. However, at some point, my thoughts get out of control before I realize their coming and the emotions and thoughts get away from me.

I was so torn up one day that I had to call my doctor. I couldn't focus. I couldn't stop crying. I get so engrossed in the feeling that I'm nothing, that I can't fathom anyone else even caring about me.

I'm reading 'Codependent No More'. It's a very good book. I see myself everywhere in it, keeping people at a distance but needed someone close to love me, in spite of myself.

I must detach. You don't have to become obsessed in order to love. I cannot be sucked into others' lives. It's not my concern. I need to take care of myself. But that's hard to do when you feel worthless. How can I be so detached and still love with the same capacity? If I can't detach, does it cause hatred and resentment?

I can make myself sick just by my dysfunctional thinking:

He hasn't called me today. Maybe he doesn't want to talk to me. (Maybe he's just busy).

He's not in a good mood. Maybe I did something wrong. (Maybe he's having a bad day at work).

He's being very quiet. Maybe I'm suffocating him. (Maybe he's tired.)

He seems distant. He must not want me anymore. (Maybe...)

Etc...

I had an appointment 10-31-12. Every time I see the doctor, I feel outraged enough to be able to ask questions/talk about what happened with people who were involved. I finally talked to my mom.

I said that I needed her to be unemotional (no hysterics please). This conversation had to be based on truth and logic.

She continually skirts the issue of her awareness. She swears to have no knowledge of any problems. Yet, she admits to being aware of my depression and resentment at an extremely young age (around age 5). She told me she thought I looked at her like I hated her (age 6). I asked if she questioned me. She said 'no'. We then discussed when she started working nights and my father started to sneak into my room. Of course, I remember earlier abuse; sometimes it was during the daytime when anyone could have seen, but didn't. I inquired whether or not she asked me what was wrong when she noticed my depression at around 6. She said she thought I just didn't love her. I asked her if she ever questioned me about my emotional state. Was she afraid of the answer? So afraid that she couldn't ask her own little daughter? In my heart I know that she didn't want to know. Maybe she just couldn't deal with it. But I still deserved better. You would think that any parent would die to protect their child. Not so.

<u>Hide.</u> Don't know what to say, etc. Hey – I'm OK, you're OK (considering). And my experiences have helped to develop me into an extremely compassionate person. I care about everyone and am very empathetic. So many people have never experienced any kind of trauma (and I'm glad for them – knowing a safe world), that I wonder how they would ever deal with any kind of problem if it occurred. They aren't trained in this type of warfare. *I am a survivor.*

I had an appointment today. Every time I see the doctor, I feel outraged enough to be able to ask questions/talk about what happened with people who were involved.

My brainwashed thoughts really mess with my head sometimes… I just keep trying to be positive. Maybe I will be lovable to someone…

Last night, I had racing thoughts until 5 AM. So I guess I'll sleep better tomorrow. I miss cuddling. I had an illusion that my sister was in the next room, while I was awake. But we live in separate states. Screwy head.

My son and his girlfriend called last night. It was sooo good to hear from them. My son fills my heart with joy.

x x x x x x x

DAD WAS WATCHING ME CHANGE CLOTHES THROUGH THE CURTAINS.

x x x x x x x

MOM WATCHED WHILE MY BROTHER ABUSED ME, WHIPPED ME, STOLE ALL MY FOOD, ETC. SHE DIDN'T DO ANYTHING TO PROTECT ME. THERE WAS ALSO A RAPE AND SHE JUST WATCHED WHILE MY HEART BROKE.

*****

February has always been a hard month for me. Brings back memories of my birthday party when my cousin raped me at a family function when I was a small child. Bad dreams. Cutting. When will I get through all this s**t.

I talked to my son several times. He started college and it sounds like all is well.

My surviving cat's so funny. In the kitchen at the counter at his home, he jumps on the counter, then onto my shoulder. And he gives Eskimo kisses with his nose.

Depression. Cut my wrist. Burn my arm. The internal pain won't stop without external pain. I'm 53 and still have these issues.

Kyle told me I needed to lose a few pounds. I told him there is a reason they diagnosed me and approved my disability. He started talking medically to me. I told him I already had a doctor. TV show – sex addiction, child abuse, relationship addiction.

I told Kyle I've had approximately 100 sexual partners - addictions and around 12 proposals. My childhood was so f**** up. I need to write details. Finish later. Can't do it now.

Compulsive love…?? It's like I'm addicted to love. I have to have someone that loves me all the time or I'm worthless.

****

DAD FORCED ME DOWN AND RAPED ME OVER AND OVER. I WAS ON THE FLOOR ENCASED IN IN HIS EJACULATION, STICKING TO ME AND POOLING ON THE FLOOR. EVERY TIME I MOVED, IT STUCK TO ME, WAS THICK, AND LOOKED LIKE A WEB. MY SISTER WAS STANDING ON THE OUTSIDE WITH A LOOK OF HORROR ON HER FACE. BUT SHE KNEW SHE

COULDN'T DO ANYTHING OR HE'D GO AFTER HER, TOO. HORROR. WE WERE BOTH ADULTS IN THIS DREAM.

*****

It's 3:05 am. I should be sleeping. I think it's because I messed up my meds and now that I got them straight again, my system is messed up. I feel really dehydrated. I'm going to drink lots of water. I hate the tremors. Bad headache. Ate a sandwich. Death sounds good sometimes. Not much to be here for. Maybe my purpose in life is over. Do I have one. Maybe I just don't know what it is. Try to sleep. It's 4:10 am.

The cutting and burning addictions are hard to stop – the addiction doesn't just go away. Snapping the rubber band on my wrist doesn't help me. The pain can't be relieved without blood or blisters. Physical pain is mandatory for pain release. Without that there would only be weed or some other type of oblivion to cover the pain. Later – I haven't done it in quite a while, but it's hard not to when I'm in an emotional uproar, all internal.

I know God is with me. I know he understands my pain. I feel it in my heart that for every experience in my life I have learned something and that for everyone I meet I gain more knowledge. This lifetime I'm definitely gaining more of an abundance of knowledge.

Praise God – I'm alive. I just went through the most harrowing experience in my life. I think I was delivered from death's door. I lost at least three months of my life and don't want to lose anymore. And I just realized it like a slap in the face.

Thank you Lord for letting me live. When I got home from the hospital, I forgot that I had a son and grandson and sister. I was IN THE MOMENT as far as my memories. I couldn't see past the front of my face… With the withdrawal of all my meds and, after several days, starting up new ones was a killer. Brain fry.

Forgot to call my sister on her birthday. My bad… Called the next day. My bi-polar seems to be acting up and I can't sleep.

Mom gave me some money to help with my bills. I'm sure my stepdad blew a gasket. This was when I was in the hospital still.

It's almost Christmas and I'm broke. No tree, no presents, less pressure. It seems like I have no control over anything. But I intend to try to straighten out my life. I need to know a man well before getting emotionally involved, if I can.

A childhood crush called me. The last time I saw him, we were making love in a corn field next to a little white church. Awesome! But when he found out how many times I've been married, he got scared.

I WAS AT THE NEIGHBORS' HOUSE. I WAS ABOUT 12. SOME WERE GOING TO TOWN. I DIDN'T WANT TO GO. I FELT OUT OF PLACE. IT TURNED OUT EVERYONE WAS GOING. SO I WENT. I DIDN'T KNOW WHAT TO WEAR. I KEPT CHANGING. NOTHING WAS RIGHT. I WAS AFRAID OF BEING MADE FUN OF. I DIDN'T FIT IN.

WHEN WE GOT TO TOWN, CLASSMATES WERE STANDING IN SMALL GROUPS. THEY LOOKED AT ME THEN TURNED AWAY. I'D NEVER DONE ANYTHING TO ANY OF THEM. I JUST DID'T FIT IN.

WE WERE BACK AT THE NEIGHBOR'S. THERE WAS STUFF ALL OVER THE FRONT YARD – TOYS, ETC. I FOUND A DOLLAR BILL. I KEPT IT. I FOUND MORE SMALL WADS OF BILLS. I DID'T KNOW WHO THEY BELONGED TO SO I KEPT THEM. BUT WHEN I SAW A DEPOSIT SLIP CLIPPED TO SOME CASH, I LEFT IT. I KNEW IT BELONGED TO SOMEONE.

I WAS AFRAID TO GO HOME – ALWAYS AT THE NEIGHBORS'. WHEN I FINALLY DRUG MYSELF OVER TO MY FAMILY'S YARD,

I FOUND MY DOG (CURRENT) HANGING IN THE FENCE, DEAD.
I FELT GREAT AMOUNTS OF FEAR FOR HER.

I WOKE UP.

At work, I feel out of place – again I don't fit in anywhere. I also feel as if no one here likes me. I had to call Boyfriend #2 and make sure he still loved me. I don't know about the people at work yet.

Me - Lost soul, Old soul, Pain, Fear/Phobias. Never ending sadness, Meds, Disoriented, Distortive Thoughts, Dissociation, Forgetful, In limbo, numb, too young to know and too old to care. How far will I go? How much do you know? Get you soul's eye out of my mind. Get your smile out of my heart. Brought me to tears but it's too late now. My other half, lover, keeper, friend, If not together it will never end, Cut, Sorrow – Deep Denial. Disjointed ramblings of a deranged mind.

Chapter 32

Letters to the Dead

In many cases, the perpetrator(s) is unreachable – deceased, missing, unapproachable, etc. In these situations, many therapists suggest letters (even if you don't mail them). You can keep them, send them, burn them, etc.

Dad - You are the most disgusting piece of sh** that ever roamed the earth. What a degrading low-life! Don't even make the mistake of thinking you're a man. You're scroungier than mutilated road-kill. No one with your lack of morals and integrity should even be allowed to live.

Don't you realize that you completely killed the innocence of a child? I will never have any self-confidence because of the result of your un-fatherly actions. You murdered my sense of self-worth. You obliterated my trust in any human being – forever!

Dad - I suppose you're really proud of yourself. You jack a**, son of a b****.

Dad – You chase me and haunt me every day following my sleepless nights. You are a monster of the worst kind. I should have been able to love and trust you more than any man in the world. But, when I can't trust my dad, it robs the trust away that I could have had for anyone – for eternity. If I begin to attempt to build trust with anyone, my fears continue to haunt me. Doubt creeps into my soul time and again. You absolutely massacred my self-confidence. And letting your friends watch!! You stupid b*****d.

Dad – I wish you could realize how warped I am due to your actions. My diagnoses are: Major Depression, Bi-Polar II with

Psychotic Features, Chronic Post Traumatic Stress Disorder (PTSD), Schizoaffective, Suicidal Tendencies, Self Mutilation, Dissociation, Agoraphobia, Diabetes II, Lymphocytic Colitis, Essential Familial Tremors, Left Bundle Branch Block- LBBB (heart issue), panic/anxiety attacks, hypothyroidism. Doctors have estimated my depression began at around 5 years old.

I will probably have problems with these issues for the rest of my life. **The Harvard Medical reports that these issues deform a child's personality and cause character damage**. Oh joy. What a legacy. I hope you're very proud. You really f**** this one up –you a******.

Dad – You perverted piece of sh**. When you can pick up a woman, why would you abuse me? You're so f***** up. You piece of sh**. You have ruined my life. Look at all the things I gave up because of no self-esteem. What I could have accomplished if you had been a normal, loving father. The only father I have is my Father God in Heaven. I just have to try to live normally, and realize that He is in charge and will mete out the justice.

****

Through all my experiences I've learned to never allow anyone else to be in charge of my destiny. If you were dealt a bad hand in life – keep your faith, re-shuffle, and re-deal. Life's continuing saga…

References

Where to go for help:
Call for immediate help:
911

Local (Denver) Numbers to call for assistance with rape and/ or assault:
720-977-5172

Blue Bench (Denver):
303-329-9922

Call your local police and ask to speak with a Victims' Advocate.

Tell a teacher or a friend or another adult that you trust.

Printed in the United States
By Bookmasters